What People Are Saying About
TIME GONE

I have spent years encouraging people to GET MOTIVATED and have SUCCESS in their lives. Speaking to packed arenas and stadiums I have shared my success formula, wisdom and secrets with over 4 million people in the last 30 years. In addition I have brought to the stage Presidents, Heads of State, Superstar Athletes, Movie and Television Stars and the Elite Business people in the world to also share their knowledge, formulas and secrets for success. Today I am happy to bring you another piece of the puzzle as I wholeheartedly recommend Jack Alan Levine's new book *TIME GONE* for its relevance, truth and impact. In it Jack shares his wisdom, knowledge and expertise accumulated over decades. It will enrich and inspire you to get the most out of every area and aspect of your life. Jack's writing will bless you spiritually, emotionally, physically and professionally. *TIME GONE* will teach you how to live the best life you possibly can, and insure you discover how to get the most out of life and at the same time learn to give of yourself where it matters most. *TIME GONE* will ignite you, encourage you, equip you, engage you, accelerate you and propel you to making the most out of your life! Read it now, GET MOTIVATED and SUCCESS will follow!"

PETER LOWE
PRESIDENT AND FOUNDER
PETER LOWE INTERNATIONAL
GET MOTIVATED, SUCCESS SEMINARS

TIME GONE is like having the keys to the universe as it answers questions and shows you how to live. A must for every young adult, this is stuff you wont learn in college, but is probably more valuable. Jack always has sage advice and a fresh perspective accumulated from a lifetime of living. Jack offers refreshing guidance, encouragement and life lessons with amazing clarity and wisdom. Words to live by! Jacks observations and wisdom will make your life easier and better... that's a guarantee!"

Dr. James L. Davis
President
WORLD LEADERS GROUP, INC.

JACK ALAN LEVINE

TIME GONE: Wisdom for Living
By Jack Alan Levine

Published by Great Hope Publishing, Coconut Creek, Fl

www.DontBlowItWithGod.com
www.LifeSolutionSeminars.com
www.GreatHopePublishing.com
www.JackAlanLevine.com

Email:
parklandjack1@aol.com
connect@LifeSolutionSeminars.com

© 2016 Jack Alan Levine. All Rights Reserved. Printed in the United States of America. Excerpt as permitted under the United States Copyright Act of 1976, no part of this publication may be reproduced or distributed in any form, or by any means, or stored in a database retrieval system, without the prior written permission of the copyright holder, except by a reviewer, who may quote brief passages in review.

Neither the publisher nor the author is engaged in rendering advice or services to the individual reader. Neither the authors nor the publisher shall be liable or responsible for any loss, injury, or damage allegedly arising from any information or suggestion in this book. The opinions expressed in this book represent the personal views of the author and not of the publisher, and are for informational purposes only.

Many of the various stories of people in this book draw from real life experience, at certain points involving a composite of stories. In some instances people's names have been changed in these stories to protect privacy.

ISBN 978-0-9904097-4-8 - paperback
ISBN 978-0-9904097-5-5 - ePub
Library of Congress Control Number: 2016945059

Scripture taken from the HOLY BIBLE, NEW INTERNATIONAL VERSION®. Copyright © 1973, 1978, 1984 Biblica. Used by permission of Zondervan. All rights reserved.

Scripture taken from the New King James Version®. Copyright © 1982 by Thomas Nelson, Inc. Used by permission. All rights reserved.

Scripture taken from The Message. Copyright © 1993, 1994, 1995, 1996, 2000, 2001, 2002. Used by permission of NavPress Publishing Group.

Contents

DEDICATION ix
INTRODUCTION. xi
2007: A JOLT OF REALITY! 3
1998: WHAT CAN YOU LEARN ON VACATION? 17
1999: IS OLDER BETTER? 39
2003: LIFE HITS HARD 45
2004: TAKEN FOR GRANTED 63
2005: THOUGHTS ON DYING. 75
2006: DOES ANY OF IT REALLY MATTER? 89
2008: GAME CHANGING REALIZATIONS 101
2009: LEAVE A LEGACY 125
2010: SHORT TERM PAIN, LONG TERM GAIN 137
2011: YOU COULD SAVE A LIFE 151
2012: FIGHT BACK, RESTORE BALANCE 165
2013: LESSONS I'VE LEARNED 179
2014: THE BOTTOM LINE 199
2015: LIFE ON THE MOVE 211
FINAL THOUGHTS 227

DEDICATION

I want to dedicate this book to all my family and friends who have taken the time over the years to read and hopefully take to heart the holiday letters I've had the privilege of writing and sending on behalf of my family and myself. In these letters I've had the ability to share my thoughts and views on life as it was happening. I hope you will enjoy the observations, struggles, victories, realizations, reality and most importantly, what I learned about life through the years.

At last count there were over seven hundred people on our holiday mailing list. We thank each and every one of you for allowing us the privilege of coming into your lives and for being a part of ours. Thank you for embracing us, loving us, encouraging us, inspiring us and walking through life with us. You're all a gift from God and a true blessing.

I hope that this book will bless everyone who reads it. That it will inspire you, teach you, and most importantly give you the desire to look at your own life and really crystallize what your own thoughts and conclusions are. Perhaps you too will start writing some holiday letters. If you do please make sure to add me to your mailing list. I can't wait to see your own opinions, thoughts and feelings… because after all, that is what makes us individuals… and there is no greater gift then being yourself and loving who you are and who God created you to be!

Remember —

"He who gets wisdom loves his own soul." (Proverbs 19:8)

You can email me at:

ParklandJack1@aol.com
Or write me at:
Jack Levine
c/o Great Hope Publishing
6574 North State Road 7, Suite 277
Coconut Creek, FL 33073

SPECIAL THANKS to the usual cast of characters, my wife Beth, John Rabe, Shaun Smith, Kim Leonard and Amanda Brown, who blindly and lovingly continue to work with me on my books when all I can do is underpay them and over appreciate them! A special thanks to my dear and trusted friend Stephen Beiner, whose habit of saving anything important just adds to his reputation as a great lawyer, and is also the reason we have all our family pictures in this book! THANKS EVERYBODY!!

Jack

INTRODUCTION

Each year we like to send a holiday letter to our friends and loved ones looking back at the past year and looking forward to the coming one. I put a lot of time into writing the letters, asking God to show me what He want me to share each year. These letters are extremely personal but also extremely universal. Though written at holiday time, the observations I share are a true reflection of life all year long. In them I share my struggles, joys and thoughts, which like yours, change from year to year and I'm sure mirror many of the same things you go through.

I've left some personal things in here to give you a sense of who I am – a regular person like you with all the normal victories, defeats, happiness, sadness, joy and pain that we all share. Each letter contains reflections, lessons learned, wisdom and insight that God laid on my heart that particular year. I believe these will help you with your life and have great value to you.

The letters are in chronological order, except I purposely began the book with my letter from 2007 because it felt so universal to me. It was the year of local tragedies and national anxiety. Our country was in flux. In it I share my overall views of life, which although constantly being refined as a result of continued living and experience, are the main theme throughout my letters.

In these annual holiday letters I'd ask people to stop, take stock of where they were at, and consider how they were going to move forward. I hope that by sharing these letters with you it will cause you to do the same.

Ok so let's get started and see where all that time has gone!

Jack

P.S. You're not going crazy and there are no pages missing in the book, as there were no letters written between 2000 and 2003. Also there are three references to items that have been mentioned in one of my previous books, *Live A Life That Matters For God*. I included them because they originated in my holiday letters. I figured not too bad, one page of previously mentioned stuff out of 240 pages. I only share this because I don't want you to think I am not aware of every word I write and publish. I am and I hate to be repetitive, UNLESS I AM MAKING A REALLY GOOD POINT! Smile!

TIME GONE

2007

A JOLT OF REALITY!

December, 2007

Dear family and friends,

It's with great joy that we write you this holiday season to give you an annual update in the life and times of our family and hopefully a little insight to where our hearts and minds are this particular day. It seems that lately we've been hit by news of tragedy from friends and acquaintances, from the sudden passing of a nine-year-old boy in Scarsdale, New York, as he was playing little league baseball to the passing of a father of four here in Florida, and of course a slew of national tragedies. This year we have deadly mall shootings in Omaha, multiple shootings inside churches in Colorado, and right here in Boca Raton just a few weeks ago a mother and daughter were murdered in Town Center Mall Parking lot in addition to shootings on a Las Vegas bus. All of these were within the last few months, and unfortunately the horrific murder of students at Virginia Tech happened in April, which shocked the nation.

As well it seems we have a slew of economic bad news already coming our way, (slump in housing market, rising oil prices, fear of inflation right around the corner, rising costs and shrinking paychecks).

I don't tell you all this to make you sad but just to remind you that our lives are fragile. Nobody expects to wake up in the morning and die, yet statistically we know that ten out of ten people die. We are reminded that life is fragile, seemingly short, depending on whose life you are looking at, and certainly most precious and valuable. We are reminded personally of God's view of life and God's value of what's important. God's value of what's important is never money.

I want to share with you some words written by a poet who put things in proper perspective.

> "I must remember as I forget,
> not to want for the things I deemed so meaningless
> when I faced death's door
> and begged the Lord for life and mercy
> things like money, jobs and relationships
> these are yardsticks we ourselves use to measure our worth
> never are they brought into consideration
> when the Lord considers our worth."

I've written you year after year, holiday after holiday, with some type of reminder of the wonderful nature and mercy and love and compassion of Jesus Christ that is available to each and every living soul on this Earth. God said in John 3:17, "For God did not send his Son into the world to condemn the world, but to save the world through him" preceded, as you probably know, by a more famous verse John 3:16 "For God so loved the world that he gave his one and only Son, that whoever believes in him shall not perish but have eternal life."

I have also given you some practical insight on things I have learned over the years that I thought might have value to you — all of them with the intent of my heart to help make your life better. I hope to remind you, if you don't already know, how to enjoy life and make sure that you are grabbing the laughter and love instead of the sadness and shame because they are all available but you have to choose which ones you are going to grab. Then you have to live with your choices.

I want to share with you a few things God has taught me very specifically through being a parent and watching my young kids grow up.

First, I was looking at Jackson and Talia the other day as they came bounding into the room, joyfully and happily playing with their toys. Jackson is five, Talia is three, and I realized that they had no concept of the plans that Beth and I had made for their future. They had no concept that we started putting money aside for their college educations by contributing to Florida's prepaid college plan. They had no concept that we had already started to purchase a few stocks for them such as Merck, Pfizer and some other stuff that we thought would grow and appreciate as they grew older in order to begin to build their stock portfolios with the hope of providing them a financial windfall for their futures.

Not only did they have no idea that we had done this because we hadn't told them, but even if we had told them today, they would have no comprehension of what it meant that we put money aside for their college education or that we started to build a stock portfolio for them. It wouldn't mean anything to them. They wouldn't understand and couldn't comprehend the sacrifices we had made on their behalf or the riches we were storing up for their future. They didn't even know it, and I thought that's exactly what God is doing with us. God tells us that He has prepared such great riches for us in heaven.

The Bible says that we will blessed exceedingly and abundantly more than we can ask or imagine. (Ephesians 3:20) And it shouldn't be a hard concept to how much God loves us and how many good things God is storing up for our future when we see that we do the exact same things for our kids. Like our own little kids that cannot comprehend our actions or thoughts, we can't comprehend what God is thinking or doing. God says in the Bible that His ways are higher than our ways, and He asks if any of us created the wind or the mountains. As a reminder to us that He is our creator and He is in control. And so God says just trust and believe that He is doing everything in your best interests and has stored so many great and precious gifts just for you. After all He is your Father, and you are His child. He loves you so much! The Bible tells us God is pleased to give us His kingdom, and already we are rich and we have all we want. So God gave me a glimpse in my life by looking at my own kids of how much He loves us and how much He is sacrificing for us and our futures. How awesome and comforting and reassuring it is to know that!

In the Bible, Matthew Chapter 18 verse 3, Jesus says, "I tell you the truth, unless you change and become like little children, you will never enter the kingdom of heaven." What does Jesus mean when he says we must become like little children? Here's what he means. When I tell Jackson and Talia we are going to the toy store, they get so excited and happy they literally scream with joy! They love going to toy store and getting toys…who wouldn't! But you know what they never ask me? They never say, "Dad are you sure there is enough gas in the car to get there?" or "Dad are you sure the toy store is open?" or "Dad are you sure you have enough money to buy us toys?" They ask no questions and have no doubt in their father! They just believe 100% if Daddy says something then it's so… They don't have to worry about how it gets done, all they know is their Daddy said it and they can count on it. It will happen. God says we are to look at him the same way. We can count on what He says and promises and we do not have to worry or understand how God works to get the full benefit of his love mercy, compassion, joy, peace and comfort… but definitely we must believe like little children. That's the key to a joy-filled life.

Another thing that is amazing to me about the kids is that at five and three years old, they can change their emotions in an instant and they are not bound by any past emotion or any concern for the future. What do I mean? They could be crying one minute because they fell down and hurt themselves, because they didn't get something they wanted, or because something got them upset. So they are crying hysterically one second, and one split second later, if I change the subject or get them to laugh or say something silly, all of a sudden their faces change in a split second. Their emotions, their whole countenances change from hysterical tears to joyful laughter, and they truly live in that new moment going forward.

They don't think for one second about the hysterical tears they were crying one minute ago. The lesson in our lives is we are to live in the present too. It's so sad and unfortunate that as we grow into adulthood, all of a sudden guilt, shame and regret comes into our minds and our hearts and ruin the very gift of today — the gift of every breath we take and every moment we live. Fear of the future, worry, and concern about things that haven't even happened also creep in and ruin the joy of today. We are to learn from these little kids that "NO! It's about living life in the present." We should react just as little kids who haven't been polluted by the world yet, who haven't grown to understand that most adults believe they are supposed to have regret, guilt and shame to carry with them as an anchor that drowns them the rest of their lives. It's not natural…kids don't have it…they have to learn it! They're not supposed to. It's just something the world has taught us to do and forces on us.

It's not something God wants us to do because God says that all your sins are forgiven… past, present and future. And God wants you to leap and rejoice. Your salvation is assured because He's living inside of you and because you have all the wonderful blessings of a God who loves you, who forgives you, whose mercy endures to you personally and forever and whose patience is unlimited. These are not my words. They are promises of God himself! And thus like little kids we need to learn to put off the past, put off the future and focus and live in the present. If you have any doubt about God's word, I challenge you to read Luke chapter 12 verses 22-35, which are headlined "DO NOT WORRY" (in my New International Version Bible). See what God has to say about worry and how we should handle it and what we should think about it.

I realize now more than ever that time is truly the most valuable commodity we have here on Earth. It is much more valuable than money. Just like I get to decide where I'm going to spend the money I earn, I also get to decide where and how I'm going to spend the time God has given me. More and more as I get older, the words of my friend Larry ring truer and truer. He told me probably eight years ago how he no longer wanted to go out at night to bars, dinner with friends, or even Yankee games, but that what he really wanted to do was be home with his young son, Steven, watching television, hanging out, pillow fighting and all the good stuff. I have learned as well that truly the time with my family, my wife, who I love so much and who is a great treasure and gift God has blessed me with, and my son Ricky who is now nineteen, and Jackson at five and Talia at three is beyond fun. It's beyond imaginable how much fun I'm having, how much joy I get spending time with all of them, and I'm just very grateful that God has given me the opportunity to have this quality time with my family as they are growing up. But it made me think about the future. What happens when Jackson and Talia are in school full time and have lives of their own, when they would rather be with friends than with Daddy? (Oh man, that's just a nightmare, right? It never really happens, right? Smile! Or cry! Depending on your own perspective!) I realize that I need to be very careful and focused about what I choose to do with whatever time God has given me here on Earth. If I don't pick and choose to do the things that I enjoy, that bring me joy, happiness and peace, and can bring joy and happiness and peace to other people, then I've made the mistake and have no one else to blame.

I can tell you one thing for sure. I do not long for "THOSE DAYS" in the past. Oh they were great and fun, and I learned from them and we had some wonderful, wonderful times, but I wouldn't trade anything in the world for "THESE DAYS" in the present. For these wonderful, wonderful days to be forty-nine years old and to be at this stage in my life, I look back with no regret for the time spent. I am just so grateful to God for the time I've been given and whatever time I have left I want to use it joyfully for the kingdom of God and be able to love and help other people with the actions of my life. I admit I have fallen short in that area and am far from perfect, but that is truly the goal I desire to obtain. So while "THOSE DAYS" days of youth and young adulthood were very beneficial for learning and were good and fun, I feel "THESE DAYS", that this time now, is so precious and so valuable because I realize that I'm growing closer to old age than I am to young age. While I still feel like a twelve-year-old kid, and I probably still think like a twelve-year-old kid, and I hope I still act like a twelve-year-old kid — happy, joyful excited — nonetheless I've come to appreciate so much the value of a day, an hour and even a minute of being healthy and happy. I appreciate knowing that God loves me, feeling the love of my family, and the joy and love of my friends. That truly is the most precious thing next to my relationship with God, and I am so grateful for each and every breath I take.

It reminds me of the reality of my own life — the search for happiness, fulfillment and meaning. I am so thankful and so grateful that for me the void that seemed to be in my life — the longing for answers about why I was born, what my purpose is in life, and where I will go when I die — have been answered for me personally by God over sixteen years ago. And that, my friends, is why I am joyful and grateful.

My buddies and I adopted a line from a Bruce Springsteen song "No retreat. No surrender." as a motto for life. Yes, I make a big deal out of Bruce Springsteen shows, not because they are important, but because life is important. And enjoying life and finding meaning in life and fulfillment and satisfaction and contentment is important.

I do not get that stuff from a few hours of Bruce Springsteen's live music (even though I enjoy it so much). I just want to let you know I get it every day, every minute of my life and will for the rest of my life, since I accepted Jesus Christ. I get it directly from Jesus Christ himself, for the love of Christ is indeed the sweetest music and words you will ever hear. You don't need to find a scalper to pay five hundred bucks for a front row seat. Jesus invites everyone in to sit with Him personally as He promises if you accept him as Lord and savior, He will come to live inside of you and His holy spirit deposited inside of you will teach you all things. It's a great deal…and its' free. I've had it for sixteen-plus years and it keeps getting better. I just want to make sure I told you because I would hate to think you thought I was keeping all this good news to myself! (Smile!)

I'm not here to philosophize and I'm not here to tell you how to live your life. I am here to share with you whatever insight I have gained in the event that it may be of some value to you. I'm actually not here to preach to you, even though you may find that hard to believe (smile). I get to preach plenty on Sunday mornings. God has blessed me with a wonderful network of friends and pastors who let me preach at their churches on a variety of different Sundays throughout the Tri-County area here in Florida, and I'm very, very grateful for that privilege. However I share my love and thoughts with you because I love you.

I've come to see that the greatest crime in a man's life is regret about the past, discontent with the present, and fear of the future. Perhaps songwriter Elliott Murphy said it best "Hey now, baby, we can have it all if we just forget about the little pieces and let them land where they fall."

I'm reminded this holiday season of my dear friend Eddie Eade who passed away some years ago. I think about Eddie all the time, and I especially think about him when I get a little rushed and busy and crazy and seem to forget my own words about living for the moment and being joyful about each breath I take. I remember Eddie telling me a story about when he was on the operating table and they were performing open-heart surgery on him. He was in his late thirties at the time, I think, and he said he laid there on the operating table and he couldn't even take a breath. All he could think was about Jesus Christ who had come into his life and saved him years ago… and all he could think was "Holy, holy, holy" as he realized that every breath he took depended on the grace, mercy and love of Jesus Christ and that God holds the breath and the life of every person in the palm of his hand.

The important thing about Eddie's realization was not just those words and the impact they had on me regarding the value of each breath and God's gift of life to all of us. But the way he lived his life and the way he's remembered by those who knew him. He's remembered today as he lived, as being one of the most "on fire" Christian guys you have ever seen or met and as having happiness and the joy of the Lord exuding from him every moment of his life. As he was always helping others, he was a true servant with a heart for the Lord and a heart for other people and God blessed him abundantly and exceedingly more than he could ask or imagine. And he would tell you that. His ministry (which was simply living a life that was sold out to God) accomplished more in eight years walking with God then he accomplished in thirty without God. I'm reminded of him and I can still see him smiling and happy and joyful. I witnessed the great impact he had on people's lives, not just on me, but on so many others who knew him. He lived a life that glorified and reflected Jesus Christ when he came to know Jesus Christ. From that day forward he simply said, "Yes, Lord, yes!" I hope that when

I'm seeing Eddie again up in heaven and when I'm seeing Jesus face to face that people will remember me the same way.

Merry Christmas Everybody, Happy New Year and God Bless!

Love,

Jack

YEARGONE – a look back at…

2007

This was a year of remembering how important it is to live in the present. What about you? Are you living in the present? Or, are you weighed down with guilt, shame and regrets from the past? Take a moment to let go of the negative emotions from the past to enjoy the gift of today. You are freely forgiven in Jesus Christ, so freely forgive others. Take a moment to rejoice and thank God. Spend time loving and helping your family and friends. Remember, time is our most valuable commodity on earth. You are important! We need you in the game. Live in the present.

1998

WHAT CAN YOU LEARN ON VACATION?

November, 1998

In 1998, my holiday letter consisted of a variety of different notes and observations I had made during the year when traveling. Here they are.

The Thanksgiving Day Prayer

>Dear Lord, you tell us not to be anxious for tomorrow,
>but we fret all day about the future.
>You tell us to bury the past and forget about it,
>and yet it consumes our daily lives, each and every day.
>You tell us to let your joy and peace make us full,
>yet we seek joy and peace in the world.
>You tell us to trust in you,
>yet we trust in ourselves.
>You tell us to walk in light,
>yet we run toward darkness.
>You tell us to love one another,
>yet we love ourselves.
>You tell us you have paid the price for our sins,
>yet we continue to let Satan judge us guilty
>and impose his penalties on us.
>You give us the instruction manual
>for how to put together a perfect life,
>yet we cast it aside
>insisting instead we can build it better ourselves.
>Failing every time!
>Lord, you tell us to confess our sins to you,

and yet we hide them from you.
You ask us to obey,
Lord, and we disobey.
Lord we ask that you redeem us from our flesh,
deliver us from ourselves, Lord,
that we might finally see
that our own efforts
are futile and dark.
Only through you is
there life and light
and love.
Lord Jesus, we are ever
so thankful for you, Lord.
We owe you our lives,
our hearts, and our salvation.
Lord, we give thanks to you
every day, not just today,
not just on a day the world
gives its thanks
but each and every day, Lord.
And today we have this prayer —
that we may
cease being stubborn
that we may
cease trying to direct our own lives,
that today Lord we may trust you,
Father, in all things.
For you have promised us

"that all things work together
for the good of those who believe."
Father, you have asked
us to believe.
Give us the strength and courage
to believe
that we may receive
the love, joy, peace and mercy
that comes from that belief.
And, Father, for this
we are thankful
every day and
every moment.

In Jesus' name we pray.

Amen

Jack Levine

TAHOE: JUNE 1998

Well hello there. It is a new day, and I think it is still June. Let's see if there is a newspaper around. There is. It says that Sunday was June 28th, so this is Monday, June 29th. It is a little after 10:00 in the morning Tahoe time. I spent a beautiful day in church yesterday with some of the locals and some other visitors from Michigan and Jamaica. I heard a twenty-one-year-old campus crusader for Christ give his testimony. He was talking about his blind mother and said that she had more vision than anyone he had ever known. He mentioned how grateful to God he was for her and how God was moving in his life. Even though he was saved as a child, when he went to college, he started partying, getting into fraternities and getting familiar with the ways of the world. This drove him closer to God as he saw that the ways of the world didn't give him satisfaction and fulfillment, and that the only place to get it was through Jesus.

I'm thinking that it is so great that these kids are involved with Christ at a young age. The kid talked about going to fraternities, not being fulfilled by the things of this world as he started to experience them, and coming back to Jesus when he realized that only Jesus could give him the fulfillment he needed as well as the love, peace and joy in his heart he desired. It was so neat to see a young person, with God in his eyes and his heart. Exciting to see that he had encountered God In a first- hand experience and was preaching the word to other young people and giving them the opportunity to come to Christ.

I was thirty-three before I was saved, but I still don't recall too many of my friends or associates (even though I am sure that I wasn't listening) coming up and telling me about Jesus. I do recall one in particular, Dave Belson, but aside from him I don't recall anybody. So I guess that makes Dave Belson, at this moment, a shining light.

We don't know what impact we have on people. No one says right when they hear something, "Wow this was a profound moment of my life." Usually the realization comes later when they look back and say, "That was a profound moment in my life."

I remember when such and such told me about Jesus or this guy turned me on to Jesus, and I will never forget it. Well, you know the guy who did the turning on and who was the light often times does not get to find that out until he gets to heaven. So we all just have to shine for God. We sow the seeds and God will reap the harvest. If we all work together for God's good, we are so far ahead of the game. I was reading in Ephesians this morning and God was saying to forgive each other, lose the bitterness, anger, rage, and envy that you had in your life before you were saved. Forgive each other as Christ has forgiven you. Oh my God, I mean that is such a great instruction manual, and it's also a hard charge for us to do. It is a hard task and assignment. Oh my God, we are supposed to forgive everybody? Totally? Unconditionally? Like Jesus has forgiven us?

And the answer is yes, that is exactly what we are supposed to do. Only then will the love, joy, peace, mercy and the Holy Spirit flow in us. Then we'll leave the rage, bitter, envy, anger and greed factors of this world. Satan rules this world. Our problems are not with our bills, our spouses, our drug abuse, our sexuality, or our financial condition. Our only problem is our spiritual condition. The attacks made on us are spiritual attacks made by Satan, and they come in the forms of physical, financial, and emotional things in our life. Guilt, hate, anger, envy, greed, shame, depression and anxiety are just tools that Satan uses to turn us against our God, our Lord Jesus Christ.

Christ says, "Here is how you fight Satan. Use me. If you are weary come to me. I will give you rest. But use me, and put me on as armor for yourselves. You have the Holy Spirit inside of you. Use that, use the breastplate of faith and the shield of salvation and the helmet of the spirit to armor yourselves. Put around you an armor of God so that the enemy, Satan, can't pierce it. He can't pierce that armor, so if you are wearing it, he can't get in."

It's like a cop wearing a bulletproof vest. Even though he's shot, the bullet won't kill him because he had armor on. He was bulletproof. We need to make ourselves "world proof," and the only way we can do that is to put on the "Jesus bulletproof vest of life." The instructions are so clear and simple. We must forgive others as Jesus forgives us. Lord, today I pray and ask you in your sweet name, heavenly Father, God Jesus. Lord, I love you so much. Today I ask you to work on my heart, Lord, and give me the ability to forgive others unconditionally as you forgave me, Lord. Let me remember the love, the mercy, and the tenderness that you bestowed upon me, that you poured out upon me, Lord. I'm an undeserving, miserable man, falling far short of God's grace and glory and plan. And yet you died for me, Lord. You sent your son to die on a cross for me so that my sins would be forgiven, so that I would have life eternal and abundant life now. So that I would leap and rejoice and love my life. And you told me that if I had cares, Lord, to come to you with them. If I had sinned to confess it to you and, Lord, I am here to confess my sins.

I am living in sin every day, Lord, and I ask you to open up my heart and show me how to change. Change me so that I can have these tender mercies and this unconditional love toward others because I am having difficulty in the sin, the selfishness of myself in which this body currently lives. But, Lord, I know that this body is for you. It praises you, it gives you glory and I know that there is no burden you have given me that I cannot bear. I know that you are with me. I know that you started this work in me and you will be faithful to complete it. I can't offer my faithfulness back to you, Lord. I'm like

Peter who said he would be loyal and then denied you three times. I too am only useless flesh, Lord. All I offer you is my thanks, Lord, for your wonderful gift. I accept that gift, embrace it, and just thank you so much for it. Thank you for your love, dear Lord Jesus, and thank you for life.

Have yourself a great day. We are going out on Lake Tahoe in a boat. Assuming we don't drown, we will be back to give you a little more either later or tomorrow. Over and out. Thank you, Jesus.

It is now 6:24 p.m. on Sunday night, and I am sitting thinking that Satan, the accuser, wants us to stand accused and Jesus, the redeemer, wants us to stand redeemed. We have to decide which side we are on. Accused by Satan and hung guilty or redeemed by Jesus and set free, absolved of all sin, our sin debt paid by his blood.

Let me tell you about my center of the universe theory. I am at Eagle Falls in Lake Tahoe, a virtual paradise — a waterfall surrounded by tall pine trees and rock-carved mountain of stone, big green trees and hills and valleys and peaks and plateaus. I am surrounded by beautiful breathtaking scenery at every turn. At every angle you see something else. Nature screaming and exploding itself into your mind. It's incredible. So, I get to the waterfall and we are looking at it from one angle, and then we hike and climb some more to see it at a different view. Then we start to come down the backside of the trail and see the waterfalls again from yet a different angle. The beauty of it all encompasses me so much. It overwhelmed me that I sat there truly believing that in that moment of time God had brought me to the center of the universe. To his complete oneness, to a place that I had asked him to bring me. Almost like Thomas, it was as if I had doubted, as if I needed a sign, as if I needed something more than Jesus giving himself up at the cross to pay the debt of my sins.

God brought me to that place. He said, "Okay, Jack, if you need more, I am going to give you more." And he brought me to the place, and I had no doubt or denial that God's hand was there. As I looked upon it, I thought of it being at the center of the universe of this Earth. It dawned on me that God was saying, "Jack, I brought you to the center of the universe. This is it. You are at this place. Now if you want this feeling all the time, if you want the serenity, if you want this alignment with my spirit, if you want this oneness with me with God the Father, if you always want this feeling, since you always can't be here, what you need to do is make me, God, the center of your universe. Make me your life. Make God as important, as special, as realistic to you as this very moment in time — as the Earth, as Lake Tahoe, as this scene in Eagle Falls, as this mountain, as nature. As I have shown you my center. Make me your center."

If we just put God at the center of our lives, there will always be waterfalls of joy and snowcapped mountains and the sun dancing on the lake. We can always have that every day — pure joy. God says, "My joy and my peace I give to you, like nothing else you can get from Earth."

So today when I realized I had literally been at the center of the human universe, God looked at me and laughed. He said, "Ha! Okay I brought you there. Now if you want this for real, if you don't want to spend thousands of dollars and months of planning just to have forty-five minutes at the center of the universe but want to be at the center of the universe eternally, aligned eternally with God's spirit and truth. If you want to be with Jesus eternally, He is inside of you. He has deposited the Holy Spirit inside of you. Make that the center of the universe and your life will always be a paradise, regardless of the circumstances happening around you."

You know, it might be like today, a June day, with the sun shining brightly and the temperature seventy or eighty degrees, or it might be snowing in January or February. The waterfalls and the beauty are still the same. So are our circumstances in life on Earth. They may be good, bad or indifferent. The uniqueness and joy and love of Jesus is still the same, and we can have that each and every day, each and every moment, if we put God at the center of our lives instead of us at the center of our lives.

It is a critical determination that must be made by each of us individually. It is not enough for living purposes to simply accept Christ. It is, however, enough for eternal purposes to accept Christ as your father and savior. But for day-to-day living it is not enough. You must make the determination to either give your life to Jesus and have him be the center of the universe or keep it for yourself. You can't get what God gives you from yourself. You have to get it from God, and that's the beauty of it.

Thank you, God. Thanks for Doug and me up on the mountain having a moment to take time out and pray.

On another note, a buddy of mine called me. His son, who is seventeen or eighteen now, had moved to California and told him that he was possibly going to stay there and not come home. My friend was upset because he loves his son and he didn't want his son to go and make mistakes with career choices, with potential life partners, with his thinking. He only wanted the best for his son, and he was literally crying on the phone to me.

He said, "Oh you know I have had a rough day. My son said he was going to stay out in California and he has crazy ideas in his head about what he wants to do with his life, and they are just insane." I heard him crying and I thought, wow, this is one of my best friends, this is my buddy. I love this guy and look at the pain his son his causing him. Look how much he loves his son.

I told him that I have never been a parent so I couldn't comment from that perspective, but I have been a kid and I remembered myself at seventeen driving cross country to California and telling my parents that I was going out there to live permanently. I can now imagine the heartache and pain that they must have felt and the tears they must have cried that I didn't know about. And you know what? At that moment, I knew about all of them. I thought of the countless times — I wish I could just say dozens, but probably hundreds of times — that my actions and thinking have brought my parents to tears, and because they couldn't control the choices that I made, they could only tell me what they thought was best. They loved me so much they only wanted what was best for me. They wanted to protect me and make sure that I had the benefit of their experience. For they could see the path ahead and they knew what was going to happen in a lot of instances because it had happened to them already in their lives.

They were advising me and cautioning me based on reality and love, and I ignored it, dismissed it, emotionlessly cast it aside, and laughed at it. Here I am years later getting to sit on the other side of the fence and see the effect, not realizing what my actions were causing on their hearts. I came to an interesting realization that the same love that my friend had for his son, the same love that my parents have for me, multiply that by a hundred thousand and you have the unconditional love that God Jesus has for us because we are His children. We are his. We belong to Him and His love is so great that He must cry and shed tears in heaven when we respond in a rebellious way.

When we don't grab the rope He has thrown to us. When we refuse the advice and scholarly wisdom that His knowledge and experience as our creator can give us, the one who has the master plan, the one who has the blueprint, the one who has the building plans of the universe and we laugh, scoff and ignore. Oh, woe is me.

Dear Lord, thank you that you love us, that our foundation, Lord, is based upon your grace and gift of mercy and not on us and our response and smartness because we have none. We are just idiots, Lord, who are lucky to be loved. Today we thank you for that love, for we do not do what we are supposed to do, as Paul said. No, we know what to do, but we don't do it and I believe that your day of reckoning and my day of reckoning comes down to that simple conclusion that God has asked us to serve, and we are unwilling — we are selfish. We are unwilling to give up the things of this world as Peter did, as Mathew did, as John did to wholly serve the Lord Jesus. And that has to be the only point of dispute and discrepancy to be discussed. Nothing else even bears mention.

Good morning, it's Monday June 30th, and daybreak is so beautiful. It is so pretty, so fresh and pure and full of hope and gratification and everything is before you. The day hasn't started yet, and anything can happen. It is truly the most beautiful time of the day. Birds are flying, everything is just beginning, and the end hasn't been decided. The world hasn't rushed in to pull its crap on you, and you haven't had to respond. You just have that moment in time with yourself when you can enjoy yourself and your thoughts and your nature, whatever is around you, which as we know this beautiful morning happens to be Lake Tahoe. As I stare out at the glorious lake, I am just ever amazed by its presence, and that's exactly how we feel about our Lord Jesus. There it is again. Good morning, world.

NOTES FROM THE LAKE: JULY 1998

I am here at 4:27 p.m. on Saturday. I think it is the 27th of June 1998 here in the wilds of Lake Tahoe. I'm looking out the hotel room, and I literally see the sun dancing on the water, shining brightly like multi-colored Christmas lights. There are all these white lights dancing, glowing and beaming off the lake. It is so beautiful and through my window (I am on the sixteenth floor) I see mountains surrounding the lakes with snowcapped mountains. It's beautiful and I have a clear view of it.

The lake is so pretty with trees and mountains. Looking out my window if you look too far down, you just see the ground. If you look straight ahead, all you have is the mountains and the blue sky. If you look too far up, you have the sun in your eyes blinding you. But if you look at just the right angle and not too far up and not too far down, you don't see the ground and you don't see the sun. All you see is this clearly framed beautiful drops of sunlight dancing on the water, trees, and mountain — a clear shot of the blue sky and the American flag waving on top of Harvey's hotel. It is just so beautiful.

So the issue here is — is life the same way? Is it just a question of how we look at things? What picture frame are we looking at the world in? If we look down at it, there is just the ground, clearly causing us to miss the beauty that lies straight ahead. So we have a distorted view and ruin the picture. If we look too far up, the sun blinds us, same problem, ruined and distorted picture. But if we look at it right, we've got perfection. We get that perfect angle, perfect glimpse (where you don't get the sun blinding you and you don't have the ground in the picture) and all you have is the lake, the mountains, the beautiful sky, the trees, and the sun dancing off the water. You've got perfection. See, you can't change the sun being on top or the ground being on the floor, but in order to see all this good stuff, you just have to look at it the right way.

What angle do you want to look at life? If you want to look at it from an "it's no good" angle, it won't be good. If you look at it from an "it's going to be good" angle, it's going to be good. The picture is there for the framing. How are you going to frame the picture for your own life?

I think everybody deals with this question. I think if you know God is the key — that He owns heaven (the sun) and will protect you from hell (the ground that ruins the picture) — you can focus purely on the middle and get all the joy and pleasure. I know it for a fact because I did it today. I went into the mountains, laid on a stone, and watched a magnificent waterfall and the beauty all around me. One of my friends, Mary, said to me, "If anyone ever doubted there was a God, all they would have to do is take a look at this and they would be convinced." And she was right. We know God's up there, God's taking care of everything. He loves us.

It is just a shame that people need and demand proof. Jesus said, "Blessed are those who do not see and believe." Those who do not ask for proof, who just believe God, do what God says and don't challenge God. They will be truly blessed. Either way, as long as you get there, it is still good. So, we had the perfect view, the perfect clear place, and I said to my friends, "This is the place I wanted to be all those days when we were riled up and stressed out working." I thought of coming to this place, and I was there. It was perfect. It was serenity. It was beautiful. It was God inspired. It was peace. It was joy and I couldn't have picked better friends to share it with. It was just wonderful. So that place exists, the key question is how often do we go there? How often do we go off into the good places where we know things are good, both physically in our lives and emotionally in our psyche — in our minds? And the key to happiness is to get to that good place as much as possible. That is what it is all about, and God is the good place. That good place exists in the heart of every person who has the Holy Spirit of God living inside of him. Today we are at the good place and we thank God for that very much.

NOTES FROM NEW YORK: JUNE 19, 1998

I had been having back pain, sciatic pain, shooting down my right leg for a number of months. In addition, I was turning forty and had tremendous business pressure on me, as our company was strapped for cash and debating whether to go public in a stock offering. With such a public stock offering comes enormous change of responsibilities and lives as well as additional pressure. In essence, I felt I had the weight of the world on my shoulders.

I flew to New York City to see Dr. John Sarno, a renowned back care specialist at the Rusk Institute of Rehabilitative Medicine.

I had been saved since 1991, and had recently wanted to dedicate my life to serving God totally. But, I had yet been unable to do so. I had done some good things on behalf of the Lord. I had shared my testimony and hopefully planted some seeds of salvation along the way to assist others. But, nonetheless, I believed I was falling short of God's plan for my life.

I had time between my two appointments with Dr. Sarno. The first was at 1:30 (for x rays and exam) and next one was at 5:30 that evening (for diagnosis). In between, I found myself standing on the corner of 34th Street and 2nd Avenue in New York City.

Normally, I would have gone back to my hotel in mid-town, the Sheraton Hotel on 53rd and 7th. But, President Clinton was in town that day, Monday, June the 8th. Therefore, there was a gridlock in New York City traffic. It would have taken me an hour to travel to the hotel, instead of the normal fifteen minutes, and then another hour to get back — in essence, a wasted trip.

So, there I was, standing on the corner of 34th and 2nd with nothing to do and nowhere to go. I immediately started to panic. I thought of who I could call, what I could do, where I could go, how I could possibly manage to kill all of this time. At that point, I prayed. I prayed to Jesus that he give me guidance, give me direction, and help me. I prayed for a long time about a lot of things. God laid on my heart just to stand there on the corner.

There were steps leading up to a patio of a church on the Northeast corner of 34th and 2nd. I went up the steps, stood on the patio, and for the next two hours watched New York City whirl by me. People walked at an extremely fast pace — rushing, yelling, screaming — taxicabs honked, police whistles blew. It was life going on around me at a very, very fast New York pace.

I studied the people, some of them in particular, and one of them an old gentleman, who had to be at least ninety. He walked very deliberately and slowly with a cane. He wore a little beanie hat, a suit jacket, a pair of pants, white walking shoes, and a bright red scarf. I couldn't help but notice his deliberate steps, and I began to think about him and his life — all his ninety years and how, compared to him, I was a very, very young man. But, here I was, concerning myself with issues of age and mortality and, in effect, complaining to God about how I was unsatisfied with my life and asking for other things I wanted.

I watched as the man deliberately walked very slowly; he couldn't go any faster. Then, he came upon a banana peel on the sidewalk and, with all his strength he reared back, swung his stick, and hit the banana peel cleanly off the sidewalk into the gutter. Content with his accomplishment, he proceeded to walk on down the street.

I believe the Lord put that man in my life for a very specific reason — to give me a very unique perspective on just what was wrong with my current way of thinking.

It suddenly dawned on me that life is a gift from God. A free gift. It says in the Bible that our lives are so short that we are merely a vapor, a mist, here for a moment and then gone.

I saw all the people swirling by me on foot and by car. I looked at the office buildings and envisioned the millions of people in them. I imagined their lives going on about them and I thought of the old man who has just walked by. I saw a young mother walking with a little baby, and I thought here is the entire spectrum of life — the young, the middle aged, and the old. God gives us life. Life is a gift from God. Life isn't something we choose. We don't get to decide how long we get to live; we don't get to decide who we are or what we look like. Those are God's choices. It's God's gift, and aren't we the most ungrateful people in the world, to complain to God about our circumstances and our lives?

It dawned on me that, instead of being aggravated at turning forty, I should be leaping and rejoicing as the Bible says. I should be grateful that God had given me forty wonderful years to experience life. Whether He chooses to give me one more day or fifty more years should be of no concern. My job is to let God know how much I love Him and how grateful I am for this wonderful, precious gift of life He has given me.

God has placed the power of the Holy Spirit in us to guarantee the treasure of eternal life — life with Him forever and ever after this world expires. But that's not all. He has also granted us an abundant life now. Who am I to say to the creator, to the potter, to the master, to the giver of the gift, "This is not acceptable. I don't like your gift. I want to change it. Why didn't you give me something else?" Only an ungrateful person or spoiled child would respond in such a manner.

I had this wonderful blessing of God's grace and peace come over me on that very busy New York City street corner. As I sat and stood for those hours and watched the world go by, I realized that God was my world and that God is my world. I realized I had been ungrateful and wrong in my thinking and attitude toward my life. I learned life is a gift from He who is most on high, He who is most wonderful.

I made the decision to commit myself to that understanding and to remember that things may not always go my way. My back pain may or may not get better. I am going to have problems in this world. After all, Satan still is the ruler of this world. But God claims that He will give us no burden greater than we can bear and that all things work together for those who love Him and He has assured us victory over Satan.

I left my dogs with a friend of mine, a co-worker, for the four days I went to New York. One of the dogs had a very nervous reaction to a change in his environment. He had begun going to the bathroom on the carpets and chewing his tail and paw until the skin turned raw. Obviously, he was very upset by this unplanned and unknown change of circumstance in his life. I, as the "father" of these dogs, knew I was acting in their best interests. I had left them with a responsible person. I knew exactly when I was coming back to retrieve them, and I knew there was nothing to worry about. But the dogs didn't know my plan. The dogs didn't know that I was coming back on Thursday to greet them. The nervous dog thought that everything had changed and his life was upside down. He panicked, freaked out, and reacted by tearing himself up — inside and out.

I thought, "Oh my God, don't we humans do the same thing? Don't we respond the same way the dog did when circumstances change in our life, when unplanned events come our way, when things occur beyond our control, or when events happen that we are not happy with? Don't we become nervous, frustrated, and angry? Don't we react irrationally and tear ourselves apart emotionally and physically?

All the time, God, Jesus the Father, knows the plan and He would never, never do anything that wasn't in our best interests, that wasn't for our best good, even though we, at that time, might not realize it because we don't have access to the Father's plans. The good news is… we do have access to the Father and it doesn't get any better than that.

At that moment, I could no longer contain myself. God's glory, grace, mercy and love were so overwhelming that all I could do was cry. I rushed into the men's room, closed the door, and burst into tears of gratitude, love, thanks and praise for our Lord and God Jesus.

My emotions were the culmination of the realization that my life was a gift and I just needed to be grateful to God for that gift. I realized that I wasn't the one who controls my life and determines what happens to it. I am so lucky to have this gift. Some people die as children, some are never born, some people have other catastrophes that they must bear in order to give glory to the Lord. The Lord has blessed me and I just wanted to tell Him — to let Him know how grateful I was for that blessing.

From now on, even though I am still human and can be subject to a bad moment or a bad day, I want to live my life truly dancing with life, dancing with the Lord, praising Him and thanking Him, not fighting him. I want to be a friend, not a foe; a confidante, not an opponent. I want to leap, rejoice, and dance with the Lord because that is how He intended life for his children to be. I am his child and, today, even though I have been saved for seven years, I realize more and more just how much the Lord loves me, how wide and magnificent and gracious His love is, how I will never be able to understand the magnificence of the Lord. I can certainly appreciate the magnificence of his love, grace, and mercy.

In this one instance, in this flash, in this twinkling of an eye, in this short trip north, God refocused my thinking. He reaffirmed my beliefs, He showed Himself again to me thoughtfully and clearly. He clearly gave me the direct path to happiness, mercy, grace, and love. Very simply, that path is accepting the free gift of life, mercy, salvation, love, joy and peace that comes from a personal one-on-one relationship with Jesus Christ. And, after you have it, and if you have it, remember not to fight it, not to question it, not to play God yourself, in which you decide what you want and you tell God how things should be. But, instead, forever be grateful to His mercy that He gets to decide how things are.

My prayer tonight for myself and for all of you is that we all go and pray to God that we are able to live for Him and not to ourselves.

Love,

Jack Levine

Boca Raton, Florida

YEARGONE – a look back at...

1998

1998 was a year of refreshed perspective. With vacations in Lake Tahoe and New York and an intense look at life at Thanksgiving time, God changed my perspective yet again, on what is truly important in this life and what is not. You see, life is about nurturing healthy, loving relationships. We are making memories with God as our Heavenly Father and with our family and friends as we share and care each day. How is God speaking to you about your perspective in life? What is most important to you? No matter what we experience in this life, we can always thank Him for the gift of today. Smile, God loves you!

1999

IS OLDER BETTER?

December, 1999

Hello My Friends,

A few things I want to share with you. I had one of the greatest experiences of my life this year, and that was the pleasure and privilege of getting to spend time with my 103-year-old grandmother and my mother and father. Last September they moved down to Boynton Beach, Florida, from Yonkers, New York, and for the first time since I came to Florida some fifteen years ago, I had the chance to spend some quality time, not just a few days here and there rushed on business or pleasure trips to NY.

An amazing thing happened. Every Sunday afternoon I would make it a point to go and play cards with my grandmother. Casino was the game, for those who know about card games. We would play for two or three hours. Grams is 103 and while she's not running marathons around the block anymore, you can rest assured she is still as sharp as ever. And what a privilege and pleasure this has been to be able to get to know her again personally, to be able to share her laughter and feel her warm hugs and kisses again. The aroma of her sweet breath as she breathes, and the smell of her soft skin as it hugs me is one of the most priceless experiences of my life. This card game Casino requires strategy and even a little bluffing from time to time. On certain instances, when I have "bagged" Gram by bluffing her in the card game, she has turned to me and made some comments that I will cherish for the rest of my life. At the very moment she knew that she had been "bagged," you saw the look of horror in her eyes. She would laugh, giggle, and vow to never to be tricked again.

Getting to hear Gram laugh like a little school girl is one of the greatest experiences I have ever had in my life, and it is a reminder to all of us who have parents, friends, and relatives who are older that while their bodies may certainly fade away and may not be what they once were, their minds are still up there. I think that often we tend to push the elderly away in fear that perhaps they don't have anything to tell us or maybe we are just scared. Maybe it's just easier to deal with them by not dealing with them or perhaps it seems harder to communicate with them as they get older. Just because they can't hear so well any more doesn't mean they can't think so well anymore.

But I will tell you this — a true treasure is locked in the mind of every old person. There are memories and stories and joys in all of them, and somehow, with God's help, if we can draw those out, we are not only doing them a favor but we will receive a blessing one hundred times over. God tells us that gray hairs are to be worn with honor for they are well earned. And I tell you this holiday season, you can take all the gifts you bought in the store and burn them and throw them away because you know what? They are worthless. All they will bring is a quick fix, temporary pleasure and they too, like every other material thing in this world, will wind up in the garbage heap in the days, weeks, and months, and years to come. You know it and so do I.

The true treasures in life, the true gifts in life, are the memories of the joy, sharing and caring and time that we spend with each other. The greatest gift you can give someone else is you — your time and yourself. And you know what? Not only is it the gift that keeps on giving but it is a gift that they will remember far, far, far beyond the time when all the wrapped Christmas gifts have long disappeared, rotted and have been outgrown. When I think of the true treasures in my life, I think first of God and secondly of the wonderful people, family and friends in my life who love me, support me, and encourage me. Hopefully I can do the same in return. That is what this life is all about, living and giving of each other. So my friends, this holiday season, give the gift of yourself, call up a family member, go over and visit, invest a little time in somebody else, with nothing asked in return. Rekindle a relationship with a family member, get to know a friend again, spend a little time — whether it is a breakfast, a card game, a ballgame or anything. It is time well spent. Trust me on that.

I wish you all my love and all of God's best this holiday season.

Love,

Jack

YEARGONE – a look back at…

1999

A year of appreciation for the wonderful people in my life, especially my 103 year old grandmother (who passed away a year later at 104). Take time now and think of all the people who have influenced your life, given you joy, taught you valuable life lessons, cared for you and loved you. I hope there are many, but even if it was only one.. be grateful to God for those people. As well remember that's the kind of person you want to be for others… someone they will treasure and remember. You do it simply by loving them! What a blessing. Remember to be the blessing to other people!

2003

LIFE HITS HARD

December, 2003

To Our Beloved Family and Friends,

Merry Christmas, Happy Hanukkah, Ho Ho Ho! It's Christmas time in the city (and in the sunshine state). Thank God for sunshine and the sunshine state… I can't believe it's been eighteen years since I got on the highway and headed south to Florida. Oh, how grateful I am for God's hand in that change in my life! What a great ride it has been, and it just keeps getting better.

As always, we send our love at holiday time and tell you what a privilege and pleasure it is to be alive, to know you, and to be able to count you among our friends and family. We are grateful for your friendship and your love, and we hope we return at least an equal amount of friendship and love to you. This holiday season, my family is praying specifically for our friends and family, that you may know the true peace and joy of the Lord, receive his full blessings and be happy and healthy.

I didn't feel like sending out the usual holiday update this year. I wanted to do something different. So, on that note, I've enclosed a few things I've written for you to read. I really wanted to share with you some thoughts I've had since I left the TV Production company (I founded in 1994) six months ago. I've had some time to reflect and think about life, justice and the American way, and I have come to a couple of conclusions and what I perceive to be an interesting thought process that I would like to share with you in the three stories that follow.

We love you and wish you all God's best. Happy Holidays! Love,

Jack, Beth, Ricky, Jackson …
…And the new "little guy?" due in June

YOU DON'T HAVE TO BE JEWISH TO LOVE LEVY'S RYE OR THE LORD! (BUT IT DOESN'T HURT!)

Now it's interesting because sometimes I think it's not enough to just tell you what God is doing in my life and share with you the messages God lays on my heart. Especially if you are at the point in your own life where you are searching and/or questioning if you should have, or if you do have, OR WHAT WOULD BE, THE VALUE OF HAVING A RELATIONSHIP WITH GOD. But regardless of where you are in your walk or what you believe today, I would urge you (especially if, like me, you are an adult who did not at one time have a true relationship with God and especially if you are Jewish) to open the Bible and read in the Old Testament the first ten chapters of the Book of Proverbs. Those chapters speak loudly about having a relationship with God.

Many times my Jewish friends will tell me they don't want to know or hear about Christ. "I'm Jewish," they say. "We believe Christ was a prophet but not the son of God." And I can accept that. I believe firmly in your right to have your own belief. But I often ask my Jewish friends "based on what you do know (Jewish religion/Old Testament) why don't you have a close relationship with the God you believe in?" Why don't you do as He says? For if you read Proverbs chapters one through ten, you will see God is quite clear that every individual should have a one-on-one love relationship with Him. Each one of us has the ability to communicate with God directly and get wisdom and knowledge directly from Him. With the receiving and understanding of that wisdom and knowledge comes a tremendous and abundant blessing. Just as if you were learning to be a painter from Picasso, the more he taught you and the more you learned, the better and more beautiful pictures you would be able to paint until you too were a master painter. The more you learn, the more benefit you get; it's the same with GOD!

So while I am certain that Jesus Christ is Lord, and believe and wish everyone would see that and have the full benefit of that, I am mystified as to why my Jewish friends (regardless of what you think of Christ) would not seek to have a close relationship with the God they believe in. Don't believe me? See for yourself what your God says and your God asks. For Christians believe every word of the Old Testament is true and believe in the God of the Old Testament. We also believe Jesus Christ is His son, who is written about in the New Testament. But I'm surprised by people who simply blow off God and their relationship with God without looking and seeing for themselves. God says, "Seek and ye shall find. Knock and it shall be opened. Ask and you shall receive."

So what are we so scared of? Are we afraid that God just might reveal Himself to us and then we would know Him? Then we might have to give up the lifestyle, views, or actions that are so dear and precious to us — the very things that if we know God is for real, we wouldn't want Him to see or know about. Yeah, those!

You can't neglect to do the requirements of the course and expect to pass the class. You can't neglect to pay for the meal and expect to eat. However, I urge you, implore you, and tell you from experience that a relationship with God is far more valuable than any earthly possession you will ever have. It will bring you a lifetime of everlasting joy, peace, and fulfillment as well as define your purpose here on Earth. You will know all those things that you can never get from money, from possessions, from jobs, or from relationships.

That's right, the peace and joy you get from God is according to God, "The peace and joy that transcends all understanding." It's the REAL THING! IT'S THE GOLD! It's there for the taking and yours for the asking. If you believe in God at all, regardless of what you think or believe about Jesus, I urge you to read the first ten chapters of the Book of Proverbs (it's only about nine short pages in total) and see if God doesn't speak to your heart about how much He loves you and how He wants you to have knowledge of Him so you can be blessed and benefit more and more.

Life is short. None of us is getting any younger. If you are not enjoying the complete fruits of a one-on-one relationship with God, you are missing something — something I believe is the most valuable possession you can ever have. You can only get this gift from God. I can't give it to you; I can just tell you where to go to get it, and that is from God. There's no charge; it's free to anyone who asks. Try it. Give yourself a present this holiday season that can and will change your life. Give yourself a new life, a new relationship with the God who created you and desires to shower His love and blessings on you. It's never ever too late to turn back to God. He will restore you and He joyously awaits His children coming back to Him. Don't let your past mistakes or failures separate you from God. Don't let your fear of the future separate you from God. The time is now. If you aren't sure where you stand with God, say a quick prayer ask Him to reveal Himself to you, to show Himself to you. I challenge you to read those short chapters in Proverbs. It will probably take you less than ten minutes. Then, decide for yourself if God's Spirit is talking to you and what He is saying.

CAUGHT IN A TRAP!

What really, really amazed me, first of all, was how much my day-to-day happiness was dictated by external events. I have to tell you, it not only amazed me, but it frightened me and bothered me as well.

I noticed that when things went my way, I was extremely happy and if things didn't go my way, I was not so happy (and probably not so nice). As such, I found that which way the wind was blowing that particular day and whether circumstances went my way or not was directly proportional to how happy and joyful I was (and probably how nice I was to other people).

It reminded me, not in a pleasant way, of the times when I used to gamble on sporting events. I remember how excited and happy I got when I won and how depressed and disappointed I got when I lost. I will tell you that there was no greater rush or high than winning. Unfortunately, there was no lower low than losing. Back in my early twenties, I was subject to tremendous mood swings, based on the day-by-day success of how I did gambling. I thought that when I had come to God, over the last thirteen years, I was a more centered person, that truly my happiness and joy came from God and my relationship with Jesus Christ, which I do believe to be the case.

Nonetheless, I found recently that perhaps I had taken my eye off the ball, as they say, or lost my focus. Unknowingly, I found myself focused on the day-to-day events of life and found myself joyful when things went my way — whether it was making money, a business deal, a compliment, getting something that I wanted or a variety of other things that I perceived to be good. I also found myself sad when things that I perceived to be bad happened to me — like losing money, not getting my way, people being mad at me or blowing a business deal. I thought how foolish and unfortunate it was of me to have taken my eye off the ball, although for a very short time, and to have fallen back into that pattern of living. Then I thought how sad it was that I used to live my life this way prior to having Jesus Christ in my life. I was so grateful for the realization that Jesus Christ was and is the source of my joy and happiness. If I look for the world to satisfy me, or some possession or item to satisfy me, I'm just being foolish and selfish. I certainly do not believe that is what God has in mind.

Ironically enough, prior to this realization, I had made a list of physical things I wanted — possessions and stuff that totaled about $80,000. I thought about all the things I had, how blessed and fortunate I was, and how ludicrous that I would even think for a second that, had someone miraculously given me a free $80,000 and I got these things, I would then be happy or believe I had everything. I have been at that point in my life many times when I've had everything I wanted. I realize that is a fortunate place to be, and I know there are a lot of people who can't say that. But I can tell you, those things I've gotten have never satisfied me. Even if I got all of the things today that I think I desire, a month from now, again, I would be unsatisfied. I would want something new, desire a new gadget, toy or something bigger and better that I think would enhance the quality of my life.

I am here to tell you that is just a load of crap. "Stuff" doesn't enhance the quality of your life. People do, love does, God does, but stuff doesn't. I just thought it was interesting and intriguing to me that even though I have been a Christian for twelve years, and think that most of the time I am focused on God, I had gotten off track. I had forgotten that the true treasure in my life is Jesus Christ. That is what makes me a rich man — my relationship with God. When I focus on my relationship with God, I want for nothing, I lack for nothing. When I focus on the world, I lack stuff and I will always lack stuff.

This holiday season, I just want to remind you to, if you've forgotten, put your focus back on the Lord. In Matthew 13:44-45 God tells us, "The kingdom of heaven is like a treasure hidden in a field. When a man found it he hid it again, and then in his joy went and sold everything he had and bought the field. Again the kingdom of heaven is like a merchant looking for fine pearls. When he found one of great value, he went away and sold everything he had and bought it." I acknowledge and remember just how grateful I am to God for the joy He has given me, for saving me, for revealing Himself to me, for coming to live inside of me, for having this relationship with Him. I truly know it is everything. I look at my flesh; I look at this body I live in that I inherited from my earthly father, Adam, as we are all descendants of Adam, and I realize that my flesh will always have its desires. My flesh is greedy, it's selfish, it's impure. It will always want more. Until I'm glorified with Christ in heaven, it's a battle I'll fight every day. But it's a battle I can have victory over and you can have victory over.

God doesn't judge us by the possessions we have. He judges us by the love we have for Him in our hearts. That's the currency God uses when He measures us. Gods tells us "a man's treasure is where his heart is." Where is your heart this holiday season? By God's currency, I hope to be considered a very wealthy man. So, I hope that when you look at me, it's not for the house I live in, the car that I drive, or the possessions I have, but that you'll judge me a rich man based on my relationship with Jesus Christ. For those material things, as well as this physical body and my health and family, are things that can be stripped from me in a moment.

This holiday season, I am reminded of what is important, of what truly constitutes wealth and riches. That is, without a doubt, the love and abounding grace of Jesus Christ. The good news is that you too can be a rich man and it's free; you don't have to pay for it. You don't have to gamble. You don't have to take a shot. You don't have to risk everything. You don't have to lose anything. You can gain everything. I truly hope and pray that you will put your life and faith in Jesus Christ. If you've done that already, that's wonderful and you know what I am talking about. If not, I hope and pray for the many people I have known this year that this would be the time you truly let God into your life.

If you are like me before I came to know Jesus, you struggle and feel an empty void in your heart somewhere. You are unsatisfied with the life you are living, even though it may appear to the world that you have a great and wonderful life. In your heart, you knew better. You're empty inside. When your head hits the pillow, you are not satisfied. You question why you were born and the purpose for your life. You know, somehow, there has to be more to life than what you are experiencing. I assure you, there is. Since I accepted Jesus Christ, I have had an abundance of joy and happiness. I have a walk with God and a relationship with God that is, for me, unparalleled. I am extremely grateful to God for revealing Himself to me and for allowing me to see Him.

WHAT LESSON DID I LEARN FROM HORSERACING?
NOT WHAT YOU WOULD THINK!

As most of you know, I am involved with harness racing as a hobby. I got my license and am now a harness racing driver. I race as an amateur, which means I donate any money I win as a driver to charity. (That is the qualification to distinguish someone as an amateur.) But, I am racing in betting races at Pompano Park.

I had an interesting experience a couple of months ago. The track had just opened up; it's closed all summer and opens back up in October. I had done five professional races prior to the track opening in October. To say I was green or a rookie was an understatement.

Yes, I had learned the trade from a couple of very good teachers, but I had definitely taken a crash course. Most of the people in the business have been in it their whole lives, or at least twenty or thirty years. I was definitely on an accelerated, shortcut course to get out there on the track racing. Anyway, the track opened and it was time to race, so I bought a horse. During that first race, I made a few very rookie mistakes. They were embarrassing as well.

I would equate it to being a rookie on the New York Yankees during spring training. All the other players are watching and you are not performing well. You make a couple of critical errors, but you're still in the lineup. Then it's opening day and you make a few more errors, not only in front of the other players, but in front of fifty thousand people as well. (In my case, the good news was there were only about one thousand people.) Nonetheless, your future as a ball player is in question. Your teammates question your ability, your fans certainly question your ability, and you question your ability. Suffice it to say, my confidence level was not at an all-time high. As a matter of fact, I was nervous, unsure of myself, and a little aggravated and disappointed in my performance. I was definitely concerned about my future performance as well.

As I thought about it, a couple of things crossed my mind. First, I realized that this is what it must feel like to be a professional athlete (or at least this is the closest I'll ever get to knowing how it feels). Guess what? It's a lot of pressure when not only are your peers watching you, but the public is watching and betting on you, for real. Your performance is being evaluated every step of the way. It's no joke… a very interesting perspective. I realized I had a clear-cut choice to make. Either I had to get very sure of myself very quickly (get confident and perform accordingly), or I needed to get out of racing because I was never going to be any good if something didn't change. In essence, I was at a crossroads of my racing career. There are all these established veterans whose jobs are secure and who know exactly what they're doing all the time and they just kind of look at you. Then you screw up in front of the fans and it's a big moment of truth. It's just not enough to realize you're at that moment. I'm sure a lot of people realize they are at this moment at some point in their lives. You have to do something about it!

For me, the turning point came prior to my next race — my second race at Pompano, my seventh overall. I was talking to a friend of mine who is a well-known veteran in the business and one of the greatest harness racing trainers of all time, Buddy Regan. (I just happened to know him previously because he was the father-in-law of a friend of mine. When his daughter and my friend were still married, I got to hang out and talk to him a little. So, I knew him before I actually got into this business.) Anyway, I saw him in the paddock, (the locker room of horseracing) where the horses and drivers hang out before the race.

As I was about to go warm up my horse before the race, he asked me how I was doing and I said, "Well, I'm not really doing so great. I'm making a few mistakes and I'd like to get together with you and pick your brain when you have time." He said to me, "The horse can sense if you are nervous and unsure of yourself. That's not really good. You need to relax and take it as it comes." I thought about what he said and realized that was really what I needed to do.

First, I needed to stop worrying about things that may or may not happen on the track. I needed respond to things and take them truly as they come. Then, I just needed to relax. If I fretted and got nervous and unsure of myself, the one thing I could guarantee myself is that the horse would be able to sense my nervousness. My performance and his performance would suffer accordingly, and I could count on myself to make a bigger jerk of myself and to not be doing this very long at all because I would definitely screw it up. Or I could relax, calm down, take things as they come, and hope for the best because I did have some talent and ability (although we didn't yet know how much or how little) that has gotten me this far, and see what can happen.

Well, it was like a light switch in my head. It was as if truly God had given me the divine moment through Buddy speaking to me. I thank God for placing Buddy in my life at that point. I went out on the track to warm up the horse with a new attitude. I was calm, relaxed, and confident. Even though there were a couple of surprises on the track that night, I handled them well. I took them as they came and just dealt with them. I had a new attitude and mindset going forward and just felt like I was at a turning point. Even if I made more mistakes, it was okay because I had confidence in my ability. I knew what to do and I knew I couldn't panic or be unsure of myself because that would make it worse.

I share that with you because life is the same way.

Here you are at the crossroads of life and, guess what, if you worry about the future and worry about things that haven't even happened yet, all it's going to do is freak you out and interfere with your ability to perform today. No good can come from that. If we let past mistakes interrupt and interfere with our ability to perform today, we're beat before we even get started. It's like a baseball player. If I made an error last inning and I'm out there in the field focusing on that error, chances are when the next ball comes, I'm going to be nervous and make another error. If I worry about all the ground balls that will be hit to me in the future and how I'm going to handle them, I will probably make other errors. What I need to do is relax and focus my attention on the ground ball that's hit to me now and make the plays one at a time. If I do that, I'll be fine and I'll do fine.

The message here is that we can't let the past that is gone interrupt us and interfere with us performing (living!) in the present. It will bury us — drag us down. It's gone; we're supposed to learn from it, but not be defeated by it. We certainly can't let worry or anxiety or stress or concern about the future (in essence, our estimate of what reality will be like in the future when the truth is we have no clue) determine our path. The only thing we can do is live in this moment, the present, now. My friends, it's time to take the bat off your shoulders and swing. If you're weighed down by mistakes and failures and worries of the past or frozen solid with anxiety and concern and fear for the future, you can't get the bat off your shoulders. Instead, joyfully swing away. Swing! Hit the ball in front of you, one at bat at a time. Heed the words of Buddy Regan who said, "Take it as it comes."

We don't know what the future holds. You don't control the future. You don't control how long you're going to live and how much time you have, when your health is going to go, when you're going to die, what is going to be, what isn't going to be. It's all in God's hands, and if you don't believe it's in God's hands, you certainly must admit it's not in your hands. Either way, you don't control it. You don't get to decide what it will be. You can either fight it your entire life and be upset and aggravated about it, fret about it and worry about it, and ruin today, tomorrow and every day that you have because you are so concerned with all these things you can't control. Or you can relax and take it as it comes and deal with it as it comes because you will handle things as they come. Worrying about things in the future can crush us, as can being burdened by the mistakes we've made in the past and the missed opportunities and moments that are gone in the past. Still focusing on them now can destroy our today and our lives!

I pray that this holiday season that you will really focus on your life and living life to the fullest. If you asked me how to get the most out of life, I would tell you it's easy, my friend. You have a relationship with God because that's the only way I know how to get the most out of life. I tried to get a lot out of life before I had a relationship with God, and life beat the crap out of me. Even though I had a couple of good moments here and there, on the whole, I was a loser in a big way. Not in the way you would perceive because you guys know me. I had friends, I had a great family, I had some good jobs and I hope I was a nice guy, but in my mind I never was satisfied. I never had what I was looking for. I never knew what my purpose was, who I was, why I was. Now, I know all those things and I just delight in the guidance of the Lord and my relationship with God and the love from God I receive on a constant, daily basis.

I am so grateful that I did go off focus for a short time this year because I got to be reminded and see just how crappy life is when it's lived for the world, when it's lived to acquire a possession or an item or thing, or when my happiness is dictated and determined by random, individual events of a day. To think that my happiness and joy can be taken from me on a daily basis depending on what happens on the Earth, depending on which way the wind blows, is horrible. No wonder people are nervous, anxious and freaked out. Of course, if you have to live every second not knowing what the next second holds, that's a nightmare. But when you have the joy, confidence and assurance of your place in heaven with Jesus Christ and know that based on your relationship with Jesus Christ you have the love of God and the power of God working in your life, well then, of course you're joyful, of course you're grateful, and of course you can "take it as it comes." That's exactly the way it should be.

Your happiness shouldn't be dictated by the events of the day. Of course they add stuff to our lives and I'm not telling you not to be joyful when life is going your way, when you're winning, when you're making good money, when your wife is loving you, when your job is good, when your health is good, when your ball team wins, when you bowl well, when you play well, when you like a movie, when you're the man. I'm not telling you not to enjoy those things. Absolutely, you should enjoy each and every one of them. But, they shouldn't individually or collectively dictate whether in your heart, in your life, in your mind, in your soul you are happy or not. When life gets you down and things aren't going your way, the world shouldn't be able to knock you down on a day-by-day, week-by-week, or year-by-year basis. In other words, you shouldn't be defeated by the world and its events and circumstances. Just the fact that you are here and living life is such a gift. Of course you should go and make the best of it and strive to enjoy it. When you have the security and confidence that after you are done in this life, you are going home to be with Jesus Christ, it makes it so easy to live this life and put up with the day-to-day struggles, problems and pains that come from life. It makes it very, very easy and good. And very, very wonderful!

YEARGONE – a look back at…

2003

This was a year of reflection as I had multiple opportunities to reflect on what is truly important in my life. I was reminded that my happiness should not be based on external events and whether or not circumstances 'go my way.' True happiness is an outward expression of an inner joy and peace that only come from personal relationship with God through Jesus Christ His Son. Have you experienced this true joy and peace? If not, you owe it to yourself to explore relationship with God. I encourage you to take a few moments now to read the first ten chapters of Proverbs in the Old Testament of the Bible. Ask God to reveal Himself to you. Nothing in this world compares to a relationship with Him.

2004

TAKEN FOR GRANTED

December, 2004

To Our Beloved Friends and Family,

Happy Holidays and Happy New Year! I can't believe it is holiday time already. The time definitely goes quicker when you have kids. It just seems to fly by. I guess that's because we are just so busy!

It has truly been a wonderful and amazing year. As most of you know, Talia, our baby daughter, was born in June. Cousin Glenn (the only Dr. authorized to deliver our babies) came in from California to do the honors! She came into our lives and has brought us great joy and many smiles. She sits up, crawls and is almost talking! We look forward to that time when she utters her first words. Hopefully they will not be "trust fund!".

Jackson is great, too. He is almost two and a half years old and is talking up a storm. He says absolutely everything and doesn't forget a thing! He is the cutest little boy and brings such joy into all of our lives. He adores his new baby sister... except when Grandma tries to hold her! ("No no, Grandma. No hold Talia!") He loves to kiss her, hold her, play with her and make her laugh. Talia watches his every move, and we are certain she will be down on the floor chasing after him very soon! Jackson goes to music class every week. Ricky is in his junior year of high school and is really turning into an amazing saxophone player. He has great talent and we couldn't be more proud of him. Ricky also got his driver's license this year, along with a car. He quickly passed through the phase when it was "fun" to go to the store for mom! (But he goes anyway.)

Beth is definitely doing double time taking care of the little ones and running on virtually no sleep. She is an amazing woman, but I knew that when I married her. I truly don't know how she does it. I am in awe at what a mother's love really is as I see it firsthand in Beth's love for our three children! I truly consider myself the luckiest man alive to have God bless me with such a loving, understanding, kindhearted, Godly wife.

I was having dinner with a friend a few weeks ago. He was having some marital problems, not sure if his marriage was going to make it or not. He has children and we were talking about who would get what in the separation and divorce. He said, "I have to have my kids." As I looked into his eyes, I could see that was the only thing of importance. All that mattered were his children and at that moment I realized that God must think of us that same way. God must love us so much that we are all that matters to Him. That is why He gave His son to die on the cross as a sacrifice for our sins, to pay the price of our sin and to ensure us our place with Him in heaven. I thought how lucky my friend's kids were to have a father who loved them like that and how lucky we are to have a God who loves us like that.

There are a lot of things we can't control completely: our health, our finances, our families, our job circumstances, but the one thing we can control is our reaction to these situations. We can control how we react when things don't go our way. It's easy to be a great guy when things are going well, but how do you behave and how do you respond and how do you react when you are getting slaughtered — when your finances aren't going your way, when your health is not going your way, when nothing is going your way. That is the true test. That where the rubber meets the road and that is where the whole makeup of your life is determined. If you can respond in love to God, have trust and faith in God, you will have that peace of God that transcends all understanding. If you can't, you will have the worry and aggravation that is constant in many people.

We are excited for the upcoming year to see what treasures and blessings God has in store for us. We pray for each of you that He will touch your hearts and your lives deeply and richly as He has ours.

Wishing you peace and joy this holiday season and in the New Year!

I hope this story below will be a blessing to you.

Jack, Beth, Ricky, Jackson & Talia

TAKEN FOR GRANTED

Seventeen years ago, in 1987, I had back surgery and had a disk removed (L4/L5). I have been fine since then, but prior to that surgery and right after, I spent almost a year in bed. So, I know what it is like to lose your health and have your life put on hold for an indefinite period. Fortunately, that surgery was a success and I recovered.

Unfortunately, I have been in bed for the last three weeks with an episode of sciatica pain. (I hope and pray that by the time you get this letter I will be out of bed, running around playing softball again.) But, as I spent these three weeks in bed, not certain when I will be out of bed and in great pain, once again I try to focus on the simple things in life. Oh, how grateful I would be to have them again — the ability to get in my car and drive around, the ability to go to the racetrack in the morning and jog a horse, the ability to meet a friend for lunch or dinner. The last three weeks have shown me that perhaps I have taken many things for granted.

I think we tend to take things for granted once we have them, but we were especially reminded of that here in Florida during the hurricanes this year — Charley, Frances and Ivan. Many of us here lost power for days at a time while our neighbors to the north sustained severe damage and devastation. We take such a wonderful thing like electricity for granted until we don't have it. We can tend to let ourselves take a lot of things for granted — our health, our families, our jobs, our bodies — but you miss them when they are gone or not working properly. The moral of the story is to enjoy the things we have while they are here because, as we know, nothing lasts forever.

You know how aggravated you get when the satellite or cable goes out on the TV? Or when the power goes out? How about when your car is broken and you can't use it? Or how about when the bank is closed and you need it to be open. We just take for granted so much the abundance of things that we have. I guess that shouldn't surprise me because most of the time we take for granted the things that are most precious — our God and certainly each other. I am guilty of taking for granted important people in my life, focusing on myself, and forgetting to tell the people I love just how much I love them. But I pray that I am not guilty of that for too long and that I come to my senses and focus each day on what is important. God, who has given us the greatest gift of all, we cast aside, we use His name in vain, as if His name is a curse word, instead of glorifying it and praising Him out of our lips. I tell you what, it is a sad state of affairs that this country is in, and we as a people are in, when the entire purpose of our lives is to get more stuff to make us happy. I have found that the world and its diversions only mark the passing of time, they don't satisfy. The only thing that satisfies is the love of Jesus Christ and knowing the Love of God.

You almost have to wonder how the cavemen did it in the old days. Their lives consisted of waking up in a cave, going out and hunting for food, moving a couple of rocks and that was it. They didn't get to go on vacation. They didn't get to go bowling. They didn't get to go to football games. They didn't get to ride horses. It was a very confined and structured lifestyle. We here today, in our time and our country have so many privileges available to us. Just the ability to get in the car and drive around, most of us have a couple of days off on the weekend to enjoy some quality time with our family, the ability to have a variety of choices to eat for breakfast, lunch and dinner and not have to the same thing every day like a caveman or a poor person in another country whose only meal may be a bowl of rice or soup all day long, if they are lucky. We have a variety of clothes to choose from and wear, and when we don't like them or outgrow them, we go and get new ones. So many others do not have this privilege. We have microwave ovens and electricity, and we are able to cook. We have telephones so that we can communicate with each other. And now, of course we have fax machines, computers and scanners. It would not surprise me that if, in our lifetime, we were able to transport ourselves from one place to another simply by going into a transporting machine. If not in our lifetime, I believe it will happen in Jackson and Talia's lifetime. Man's technology is mind boggling.

All this has given us great comfort, but I have noticed that it has not necessarily given us great satisfaction. At the end of the day, I have to wonder who truly is happier — the caveman with none of the modern conveniences of today or us, with literally the world at our fingertips. I bet it would be the caveman because while we are experts at creating distractions to take our focus away from things that are bothering us, or the realities we don't want to or can't face (our families, our jobs, our personalities, our situations, etc.) those cavemen did not have that luxury. They had to focus on the problems at hand. They couldn't escape into drugs, into gambling, into pornography, into work or other things they might want to escape to. They didn't have that luxury. I believe that King Solomon in the Old Testament book of Ecclesiastes summed it up best when in his search for happiness, he availed himself of everything the world had to offer — every distraction, every diversion, every pleasure, everything you could possibly think of. He got himself not only as much as he wanted but also more than anyone could possibly want. He concluded in the end that nothing satisfied and nothing mattered except that you woke up in the morning, were healthy, and were able to eat, drink and enjoy the work you did during the day. Solomon said that everything else is vanity. Everything else is useless. That way, you went to bed with an easy, unstressed mind. How many of us can say we go to bed with an easy, unstressed mind.

Have you ever felt taken for granted? Have you ever felt that you weren't appreciated for either the job you did, the love you've given, or for some reason? Not a good feeling, is it? No, it's not a good feeling to feel that you are not appreciated or that you are working so hard or doing something so well yet nobody is noticing or nobody cares.

This holiday season, ask yourself, do you take God for granted? If you have ever had it happen to you, you know it doesn't feel very good. My next question is how long will you let yourself be taken for granted? Probably there is a time limit, where you would not continue to do what you are doing if you kept getting taken for granted because you may get angry, mad, or frustrated. You may say it isn't fair that you don't get the recognition you deserve.

Where would you be if God came to that point with you? What would happen if you had been taking God for granted and He said that He was not going to take it anymore? Fortunately, our God is a loving God. He is your Father and He loves you, and much like we took our parents for granted and they still loved us, or our children take us for granted and we still love them, God loves us no matter what. So, we do not have to fear that God is going to withdraw His love for us. But, you know what? Think of the blessings we would get if we didn't take God for granted. Think of the joy God would get and the more joy and blessings He would want to give us if we made Him joyful and happy instead of taking Him for granted.

So, this holiday season, I am going to ask you to take a look at your life. I am going to ask you to ask yourself if you enjoy each day. Are you stress free? Are you laughing most of the days? Is your life filled with joy and laughter? Or instead, is it filled with stomachaches and headaches or stress and worry, guilt of the past, worry of the future, dissatisfaction with the present, with yourself, your friends, family, job, or life?

This is not the life God intended you to have. God intended for you to have a happy, joyful life. That would not exempt you from the pressures and hardships of being alive, but it would sure be nice to know that, when you are going through these things, God is with you every step of the way. He will never leave you or forsake you. I can say that with certainty.

I hope and pray this holiday season that you, too, can say it. If not, now is the time. A new year is coming; now is the time. You do not have to continue to live that way. God has a better answer and you can find it simply by opening up the New Testament and beginning to read in the book of John or perhaps by listening to the enclosed CD. I hope and pray this holiday season that you accept the greatest gift ever given. That is the gift of eternal life given to us by our Lord Jesus Christ through the sacrifice of His Son on the cross to pay the price of our sins and ensure that we are not separated from God for all eternity in Hell, but are reigning with Him in Heaven for all eternity.

I pray this holiday season that you will look back, look present, and look ahead. Life is short and you can have the kind of life you want to have. You can have a victorious, glorious, love-filled, peace-filled, joy-filled life with an abundance of spiritual riches.

I can't promise you material riches; that's an individual blessing from God. I do know that material things are not important. God is important. I think when I made that realization in my life many years ago, God started to bless me with some material things because they were no longer a priority in my life. When God was my first priority, things started to happen for me in a lot of good ways. "Seek first the kingdom of God and His righteousness and all these things shall be added to you." (Matthew 6:33) I hope today that you will follow God's instructions and seek first the kingdom of God and his righteousness. All these other things will follow. Don't try to get everything you want and then figure you will have time for God later. That's just not how it works. Trust me — I know it for a fact. As Bob Dylan once said, "Take a tip from one who has tried."

Well, friends, we love you and pray God's blessing upon you and your family this holiday season. In Jesus' precious name we pray. Amen.

YEARGONE – a look back at…

2004

This year gave us the opportunity to evaluate our lives. I encourage you to take a moment to review your life with the following questions: Am I taking anyone or anything in my life for granted? Health, family, job? Am I taking God for granted? Am I thankful and rejoicing each day? Focus on the simple things in your life. Purpose in your heart to arise each morning thankful for TODAY, thankful for God and the people He has placed in your life. Find things to enjoy TODAY. Look for opportunities to laugh. And, remember, God is with you on the mountain top AND in the valley. He will NEVER leave you or forsake you.

2005

THOUGHTS ON DYING

Christmas, 2005

Dear Family and Friends,

I really thought I would be writing you the typical holiday letter this year — the one where I recount the past events of the year, tell you about what God has been doing in my life, what's happening with my family, where my ministry is headed and perhaps some other thoughts and experiences that have happened during the year (like Ricky getting backstage to meet David Sanborn, how amazing it is to play baseball with Jackson and Talia, how great it is to preach in different churches, etc.) But something happened to change that. I decided to share with you this holiday season some thoughts that were going through my mind when I thought my father was dying. So, we're going to go down a bit of a different path this year. Here's what happened a few weeks ago…

My dad had a heart attack last month and he almost died!

Now prior to this, I have had the privilege of Dad coming to church a couple of times to hear me preach. I have had the privilege of sitting down with him once or twice and sharing God's plan of salvation with him. He said that he wasn't ready to accept Jesus. He said that his father, who is long since dead, (I am forty-seven and I never met my grandfather) would never understand it.

Even though his father had long since been dead, you could see that he couldn't accept the fact that he would be doing something that was displeasing to his father, even though he may have wanted to and even though it would clearly be in his best interest. I could see that he was hanging on to a heritage, to a religion that teaches that the world is trying to strip away its identity. For years, history has shown us that the Jews have been in fear of losing their identity. As a matter of fact, when I got became a believer in Jesus Christ my dad said to me, "So, you're not Jewish anymore?" I said, "No, Dad, I am still Jewish. I'm as Jewish as I am white, but I have added the blessing of knowing Jesus Christ as my Lord and Savior to being Jewish."

Even though I have had the opportunity to speak to Dad a few times, he made his position clear. My father has always been a man who has believed we should "live and let live." He has always been willing to let the next guy believe what he wants to believe as long as the next guy's views were not imposed on him. So, God put on my heart to write a letter to my father. I know I will have the opportunity to talk to him and witness to him now that he has made it through the heart surgery, but I really believe that if I simply talk to him his response is going to be the same. So I decided to write this letter and I gave it to my Dad, I call it "Thoughts on Dying." Because I love and value you so much as a person, I thought I would share this letter with you as well this holiday season, I hope and pray it touches your heart and has the same importance and impact on your life as I pray it does for my father.

Love,

Jack, Beth, Ricky, Jackson & Talia

THOUGHTS ON DYING: NOVEMBER 25, 2005

Where do I even begin to share with you how I felt that day when I thought my dad was dying? When I rushed home after I got the 911 call and didn't know if I would find him dead or alive? At that point,

I went to my God, my Jesus, and I prayed and I said, "Lord, give him more time if you can, but if not, Thy will, not mine be done." And I prayed for more time so I could witness to him.

I thanked God for the time he had given me with my father. I thanked God that I was so lucky and blessed to get such a wonderful father. That applies to all my family — my mother and brother, and my wife and kids, as well. But to have a father who loves me, who sacrificed for me, who gave everything so that my brother and I could have a better life, so that we could have the things he didn't have, now THAT'S A HUGE BLESSING!

One day, when I had back surgery in 1987, I was lying in bed talking to Dad and he was complaining about spending $11,000 a year on health insurance because he hadn't gotten health insurance while he was young and now he had to get it while he was older. I said, "Dad, let me ask you a question. When we were growing up, you always gave us everything we wanted. Even though we were middle class kids, my brother and I had everything. We truly lacked for nothing. Why did you do that? Why did you sacrifice so much for us then and not for yourself?" And he looked at me without missing a beat and he said, "Because I wanted you guys to have everything." I thought, "How lucky am I? How lucky is my brother to have a father who wants us to have everything and who would sacrifice himself so, indeed, we could have everything." I just felt very blessed and very lucky. Literally like the luckiest man in the world.

Now, as I thought my father's life might be over at seventy-four years old and I wasn't going to see him again, as I thought about being a father myself and how much I love my own kids and how for the first time in my life, when I look down at my children and I see myself in them, I now understand what unconditional love is. Now

I understand why God would sacrifice His life for His children, why Jesus would die on the cross so that we could have eternal life, why He would willingly substitute himself in our place and why He would pay the debt of our sin. I understand how much He must have loved us to do that because I understand how much I love my own children now. Of course I would die for any one of my three children, on the spot. I would trade my life in an instant, if it meant theirs would go on.

Then I realized I had a big problem that day. My Dad could be dying! But I thought my dad has a bigger problem because my dad had heard of Jesus, but he didn't know Jesus personally. (For example my Dad knows who President George Bush is, but he doesn't know George Bush personally. My Dad knows who Bruce Springsteen is, but he doesn't know Bruce Springsteen personally.) It dawned on me that time had slipped by, that the last bell had rung, that the game was over and, indeed, there was no more time for me to tell Dad about Jesus. My prayer that day, I said, "Lord, please, let the guys in the ambulance tell him. Please let the paramedics, as they're going to the hospital tell him. Lord, please put a Christian in my father's life right there and let him accept you, Lord, so that he doesn't miss out. So that he goes to heaven, so that he doesn't spend eternity separated from you, Lord, but instead spends it with you in all glory." I knew it wasn't too late as long as he had one breath left. I prayed so hard that God would put a Christian paramedic in that ambulance or a doctor in that hospital or somebody so if he died, somebody would have led him to salvation. If that wasn't the case, I prayed that God himself, the joy of the Lord Jesus himself, would come to my father as he came to me and say, "It is I. It's Jesus." And my father would respond, "Yes, Jesus." And spend all eternity in heaven.

I thought what a tragedy that I failed the person I love so much. I told him about Jesus, but I always thought I would have more time to witness to him and that he would come around one day. He'd see the light. I know he sees the difference God has made in my life. One of the greatest days of my life was one day when my father was telling me how proud he was of me and the man that I'd become and the life I live. I was just thinking that it's all because of Jesus; I didn't do any of it. I don't deserve any of it. It's only because of what God has done in my life and I was so grateful.

I thought that I failed with my mother, too. I prayed that God would give me another chance, give me some more time so I could make sure, Lord, that at least when the rubber meets the road, they have another chance. At the end of the day, everybody has to decide for themselves, but I'll make sure that I don't make that mistake again. So, Dad, I ask you this… Had you died, do you know where you would spend eternity? Because had you died, you would not have the option to come back and rethink your position. Dad, I have to tell you this, if you think that next time you die you are going to be spared, you may not be so lucky again. Next time you could die. I hope it is twenty or thirty years from now, but it could be tomorrow. It could be today. We don't know the hour and we don't know the time. It's only ordained by God.

Dad, I pray that you would look deep into your soul. I pray that you would pray to God and ask him to reveal Himself to you. There are no accidents. It's no accident that I became a Christian. It's no accident that Jesus Christ is in my life. I believe that regardless of the impact and the way Christ is using me for any other people, the best thing ever would be for Him to use me within my own family. Dad, here is the problem; you can't afford to be wrong. My challenge to you today is that even if you aren't sure I am right, I challenge you to spend every waking moment seeking God.

Spend time seeking Jesus Christ. God says that if you seek, you will find. If you knock the door will be opened, if you ask, you will receive. I challenge you to spend three months studying the Word of God and praying and asking God to open His heart to you, to open your eyes and enlighten you and show you that it is really Him. I challenge you to come back to me at the end of ninety days and say, "Your God didn't meet me. Your Jesus didn't show up." Because I know my God and He shows up in a big way. My God is alive. My God's not dead. My God is not a figment of my imagination. My God is alive and God promises that when you accept Him as Lord and Savior, He comes to live inside of you. He takes out your old heart and puts in a new heart and God says in the Bible:

> *That if you confess with your mouth, "Jesus is Lord," and believe in your heart that God raised him from the dead, you will be saved. For it is with your heart that you believe and are justified, and it is with your mouth that you confess and are saved. As the Scripture says, "Anyone who trusts in him will never be put to shame." For there is no difference between Jew and Gentile—the same Lord is Lord of all and richly blesses all who call on him, for, "Everyone who calls on the name of the Lord will be saved." (Romans 10:9-13)*

> *Jesus declared, "I tell you the truth, no one can see the kingdom of God unless he is born again."(John 3:3)*

> *"Do not work for food that spoils, but for food that endures to eternal life, which the Son of Man will give you. On him God the Father has placed his seal of approval." Then they asked him, "What must we do to do the works God requires? Jesus answered, "The work of God is this: to believe in the one he has sent." (John 6:27-29)*

> *"For God so loved the world that he gave his one and only Son, that whoever believes in him shall not perish but have eternal life. (John 3:16)*

Dad, when I came to the cross of Jesus Christ and accepted God into my heart, I didn't know all there was to know about Jesus Christ. I just knew that God was knocking on my heart and I needed to respond and say, "Yes, Lord, yes." I believe this heart surgery was your last wakeup call. I truly believe this with all my heart. You may live thirty more years, but if you let this opportunity pass here, it will have been for nothing. This was God's wakeup call for you.

If anything, it got me to write this letter and to tell you that eternity is a long time and the worst thing I could ever imagine is sitting up in heaven in all the glory with Jesus for all eternity and you not being there. You, the person I love so much, who taught me so much. You know, my friends kid me because I always say that the older I get, the smarter my father gets. I tell them about the things you taught me and how you shaped and guided my life. My friend Joseph pointed it out to me. He said, "You're always telling me what your dad said." I said, "Yeah, because he always told me about these things and he was right." He told me things like "trees don't grow to the sky... When things are going good, everybody's a genius... When things are going bad, people start pointing the finger... A fool and his money are soon parted... An idiot and his ass are soon broken... Keep your head about you while all others are losing theirs... Sleep on it; things always look different in the morning... Never put all your eggs in one basket." Dad, it's great that you taught me so much and I appreciate it more than you can know.

The bottom line is that it won't matter much unless you learn something from me. I just ask you to put aside your stubbornness. I ask you why you are worried about what your father would think. Your father is gone. You know what? I think your father would want you to make a smart move. I think you would want me to make a smart move if you weren't around. You know, if you had told me something, if you had told me when we were growing up the Earth was square and that is truly what you believed 100%, but later scientific evidence proved the Earth was round, I don't think you would want me to tell my kids the Earth was square. You would want me to tell them the Earth is round now that we know it to be true.

I want you to be able to know the joy and glory that comes from an individual relationship with God, but that is secondary. I don't want you to spend eternity separated from God. I just cannot bear that thought because I love you so much. All your life you did everything so that I would have a better life, so that I would have more, so that I would be okay. I truly believe now, as I pray to God, the primary reason I was born was so that God would use me as a witness to you, so that you would give your life to Jesus Christ, so that you would be in the kingdom of heaven for all eternity. So, Dad, I challenge you to not miss this blessing under any circumstance.

I share with you the revelation that God has laid on my heart about how critical it is that you put aside the burdens, thoughts, and guilt of any other human being. You are not accountable to other people. You're not accountable to your father. You are only accountable to God, your Creator. Your father did his job. He gave you life. You did your job with me. You gave me life. You've given every bit of advice to the best of your knowledge that you can give to Mike (my brother) and me, and that's what you're supposed to do. A lot of fathers don't get that luxury with their sons. A lot of fathers die before they have a chance to watch their sons grow up or they're estranged from their kids and don't get that luxury.

You've told me that people change their minds, that's why we have to put things in writing because all of a sudden people's memories get foggy and cloudy about what they said when things aren't going so good any more. The reason I bring that up is to say to you that you cannot be bound by obligation, guilt, thought, fear or worry about what anybody else will think.

Jesus says, "If you deny me before men, I will deny you before my Father in heaven." (Matthew 25:41) Dad, we know one thing for sure. You and I did not create this universe. We didn't create this world. And the likelihood that matter randomly collided in outer space and the world was created is ludicrous. There is a God and I challenge you to seek Him out because I promise you — if you seek God, you'll find Him.

I have to believe in the fourteen years I've known Jesus, you've seen me live a better life, and I have to believe that you won't make the biggest mistake of your life. I don't mean to take anything away from the things that you've done in your life on Earth. They've been wonderful. But God says that we're a mist — here for just an instant. Compared to all eternity, our time on Earth (a mere seventy years) is really nothing. Puff they're gone! Finished! OVER! Then what?

I'm talking about eternity. If Jesus really was Lord, you're making the biggest mistake of your life, bigger than betting on Loral stock. And you know what, either Jesus Christ is God Himself or He is the biggest liar to ever walk the Earth. He didn't say he was a nice guy or a prophet. He said, "I am God. I am the living son of God." Either He's a liar or He's telling the truth, but there's no middle ground. You can't say that Jesus was a nice guy or Jesus was a smart religious figure. He's either a liar or he's God. And Dad, you can't afford to be wrong. I am telling you, as sure as I am living and breathing, I know God. He lives inside of me. I know many people who know Him. If I could ever give you anything, one gift, it would be to point you toward Jesus Christ, so that when your day comes, you will spend all eternity in heaven.

This isn't about religion; it's not about being Jewish or white. This is not disrespecting the Jewish religion and it's not disrespecting your father. It's about respecting God, your Creator. You know what? A lot of people say a lot of different things about a lot of different gods, and you believe in the Jewish religion because that is the way you were brought up. But, I just challenge you to search for the truth yourself, to pray to Jesus to reveal Himself to you. Study, seek, pray and find. Let Jesus speak to your heart, Dad. I really believe from the bottom of my heart this is the reason I was born — for this moment today, for this letter. Everything else I do is secondary. I prayed God's blessing on this letter; I prayed that God would take it and bless it and stir up a part in your heart. I pray that when you face death's door the next time, you won't leave to chance where you are going to spend eternity.

You can't afford to be wrong. Remember you told me, "When you're dead, you're dead forever, you can't come back." That's right. You can't come back to this Earth, but you can spend all eternity in heaven. Let me ask you this one question. How stupid would you be if it was true and you missed it because you were too stubborn to take a look? This isn't like just missing out on a good-tasting food. Oh, I didn't like the way that looked, so I didn't eat it, so I didn't taste it, but I have other food. This is all eternity; this is forever! I am your son; I am your blood; I am you. So, I ask you to hear what you've created. Seek God. Don't miss it.

So, these are my thoughts on dying. I love you, Dad. Merry Christmas.

Jack

P.S. In case you are having the same thoughts about sharing God with some of your family and friends and are having trouble sharing your faith with someone you know, you may want to consider the following illustration, which inspired me. It's the story of two airline passengers. One was given a parachute to "improve his flight" and he accepted it experimentally (it didn't prevent a turbulent flight and other passengers laughed at him for wearing the parachute), only to eventually discard the seemingly useless apparatus when it began to weigh him down.

The other passenger was given a parachute and told that at any minute the plane will crash and he will have to jump out at 25,000 feet.

Instead of telling people that Jesus improves the flight, we should be warning the passengers that they are going to have to jump out of the plane. It's appointed for man to die and after this comes the judgment. When man understands the horrific consequence of violating God's law (an eternity in hell separated from God), he will run to the love of a faithful Savior to escape the wrath to come!

Good luck in your own witnessing and God Bless.

YEARGONE – a look back at…

2005

This was a challenging and thought-provoking year as I faced the very real possibility that my dad could die. You know, death has a way of motivating you to filter out the less important stuff and focus on the most important issues and decisions in life. I wrote a letter to my father from my heart out of deep compassion and concern for his eternal future. Eternity is a very long time. It is way too long to be separated from the Heavenly Father who loves you. Where do you stand with God? What about your loved ones? Having a relationship with Jesus is the most important decision you will make in this life. But you have to choose it. God promises "all who call upon the name of the lord will be saved." Do not spend eternity separated from the God who loves you with an everlasting love. Seek Him and you will find Him. Search for the truth yourself. He will reward your search.

2006

DOES ANY OF IT REALLY MATTER?

December, 2006

WHAT DOES IT MATTER?

Who cares what time you get there? Who cares if you are ten minutes late or ten minutes early for the dinner appointment, for the baseball game, for the dentist, for your date, for your meeting, for your job interview, even for open-heart surgery? I mean, who really cares? Does any of it really matter? You know, when you go to the doctor's office, they never see you on time anyway. It doesn't matter what time you get there. They are always running late. And for any of you who have had a surgery scheduled, there is a scheduled time, but it never happens at that time. It happens according to the order that things transpire during the day. You could have a 10:00 a.m. surgery scheduled and not get into the operating room until 2:00 in the afternoon, depending on how things are going and the time it took for the other operations before you to be completed.

How about airports and airplanes? Do you think they really leave on time? They have the scam down perfectly. They push away from the gate by the time of their scheduled departure and they call that an on-time departure. But, the truth of the matter is that you could be sitting on the runway waiting to take off far beyond your scheduled departure time. Does it really matter?

What about phone calls that you were supposed to return in a timely manner but somehow didn't get to, due to the hectic rush, pressures, obligations and commitments of the day. What about the people on the other end of those phones and e-mails waiting for your response? Does it really matter? How about the commitments you've made to yourself — the things you promised yourself you were going to do? Get in shape, take better care of yourself, eat better, spend more time with your family, be a better husband or wife, be a better father or mother to your children, devote more time to your relationship with God. And somehow, again, in the hectic commitment, obligation, rush, worry, stress, pressure, and sometimes even excitement and fun of the world they seem to get pushed behind. Does it really matter?

At the end of the day, I don't think it really matters to anybody else. I have given it a great deal of thought. Basically, I have concluded that it really doesn't matter to anybody else. You see, everything gets done; it is just a question of when. All those phone calls and e-mails get returned, even if they are late. The surgeries get performed, the airplanes take off, the meetings happen, and life goes on, albeit, slightly behind schedule in most cases. So, I have come to the conclusion that even though I pride myself in being an on-time person, one who is usually early for commitments and obligations as opposed to being on-time or late, at the end of the day, I am no better off than those who are late. The same things happen to both of us and the world keeps moving along at its own speed, conscious only of its own desires. If my desires happen to coincide with the world, the world lets me have what I want and if it doesn't, I don't get what I want. (A little similar to King Solomon's observations in Ecclesiastes... hey what can I say... He was ahead of his time!)

I started to think about the pressure we put on ourselves to perform in our lives, to do the things we're supposed to do, as if we were highly paid athletes, rock and roll stars or astronauts, who have to be at a certain place at a certain time. Kick off time in the NFL is 1:00 p.m. When the shuttle launches at 7:14 a.m., that's when it goes. You know what they say on Broadway, "The show must go on."

We put so much pressure on ourselves to perform, to do the things we're supposed to do, to make sure that we maintain our schedule of commitments and obligations as best we can when the reality is that our efforts are pretty futile anyway. Yet we put so much additional pressure on ourselves. In addition to the pressure we put on ourselves, the world does a really good job putting extra pressure on us. Our spouses and our families lovingly, not purposely to hurt us in any way, put a lot of pressure on us. Our jobs, well, I don't have to tell you about that. You know how much pressure you have at your own job. How about the desire to get ahead, the desire to be able to secure your family's future, the driving motivation to be the best at what you do or to get ahead to make a better life for yourself? Man, that is pressure that never goes away. It's always there.

Now, I do believe that it does not take a rocket scientist to figure out anything I've told you. There is nothing magical or mystical about the observations I have made. As a matter of fact, they are pretty simple and plain. But I do think that the key to life is to be able to enjoy the ride, to enjoy your life, to enjoy the game, so to speak, as you go through it because the truth of the matter is the pressures of the world will never disappear. They will just increase and increase, so much so, you may even feel like you are a victim of Chinese water torture, or worse yet, being squeezed under the intense pressure needed to create a diamond. Or, worse yet, being fried like an egg in a frying pan.

All of these are probably pretty accurate descriptions of what we face and feel as we go through our lives. But you know what? The only way to keep score in your life is by how happy you are. That is how you keep score. It's not by how much money you have, it's not by your job title, it's not by where you live, it's not by what you look like, it's not by how good of an athlete you are or how smart people think you are. It is simply by how happy you are because none of the other things really matter. Happiness is the only thing that should matter.

So, this holiday season, as I have often done in the past (at least I hope I have), I try to get you to think about your life, about what is important to you, about what makes you happy, about what you should do, about what you shouldn't do. And I really urge you to look at your life this year and ask yourself this one question — Are you happy? If not, ask yourself — What are the areas of your life that are not making you happy? Do they really matter? Don't you deserve to be happy? You know, life is short and ten out of ten people die. At the end of the day, the only thing that is really going to have mattered is — were you happy, did you enjoy yourself, did you make the best of the life you were given?

How do you define making the best of the life you were given? For me, that is easy. I define it by loving God with all my heart and soul and attempting to glorify God by the way I live my life. I attempt to share God with as many people as possible so that I can bring the blessings and joy of the Lord to as many people as possible because I found in my own life that is the only thing that brings me happiness — my relationship with Jesus Christ. When I am focused on that, I am truly enjoying the world, the things in it, the people in it, and the love of Christ flows through me, much to my benefit and blessing. So, I am very, very grateful for that gift that Jesus has given me and it is available to everyone — the gift of eternal life that assures my place and your place in heaven and the abundant life that God so generously gives to all His children. God's true desire for us is that we would be happy, as we would wish for our own children to be happy.

Maybe you think that if you had the things you wish you had in your life, you would be happier. If you had more money, a better job, a different spouse, lived somewhere else, had a bigger car, a bigger house, looked differently, had more athletic ability, or were able to play guitar, you would be happy. I can tell you that I have met a lot of people in my life who have these things and none of them are the key to happiness. I strongly urge you this holiday season to get alone with God, to spend time searching and seeking the word of God and see if you won't agree that the definition of happiness is being filled with joy. The best way and only way to be filled with joy that lasts is to know, share in, partake in, and participate in an individual one-on-one relationship with your God, your Father, your Creator, someone who loves you so much that all He desires is to have that relationship with you. That is the desire of God's heart — to know you and love you.

You've heard people say that when you are lying there on your deathbed, no one wishes they had spent more time in the office working. As a matter of fact the regrets people have are that they did spend too much time at work and that they didn't devote more time to their children when they were young and growing up because then their kids grew up and were gone, having a life of their own. They regret not devoting more time to their wife and to their families and that they didn't spend more time doing the things they loved and enjoyed doing — golf or bowling, fishing or baseball, writing, reading, pinochle or whatever in your life gives you pleasure.

For me, that is preaching and sharing the word of God, and that is why over four years ago, I got out of the business world on a full-time basis, so I could devote my time and my life to serving God and loving God. Accomplishing what I believe was God's plan for my life has brought me so much peace and joy it is beyond description. I just weep with joy and happiness when I think of how lucky I am to know God, that He desires to bless me, and that I have a one-on-one relationship with Him. I can tell you that Jesus Christ is a real person.

My relationship with God is with a real person, the person of God, the Holy Spirit of God is real. Jesus is real. It is a real relationship, as real as my relationships with my wife and my children. I urge you to seek that person of God and know Him yourself. I promise you will not be disappointed.

So, what does it matter? I don't know if you ever heard the story of the boy and the jellyfish. One day a child and his father were walking along the beach. When they came upon what seemed to be thousands of jellyfish washed ashore, the little boy ran down to the jellyfish and started picking them up one by one and throwing them back into the ocean. "Come on back here," the father yelled to the boy. "You are wasting your time. There are a thousand of them. You can't make a difference. It doesn't matter!" The little boy held up a jellyfish, looked at his father, innocently, and said, "It matters to this one," as he tossed the jellyfish back into the ocean and gave it back its life.

You know what? Happiness does matter and it should matter to you. You are that jellyfish. You may not be able to make everyone happy, but truly there is no excuse for not being happy yourself, regardless of the situation you are in. I know people who are in physical pain who have joy in their hearts. I know people who are in financial distress who have joy in their hearts. I know people who have relationship issues, who have been divorced, whose children have turned against them unjustly, who have been robbed, who have been ripped off in business, who all have joy in their hearts because the events and circumstances of the world do not dictate their happiness or sadness. What dictates their happiness or sadness is their heart, and their hearts are joyful because they are aligned with the heart of God.

This holiday season, I have come to the conclusion that it does matter. Your life matters, your happiness matters, the way you live your life matters, who you are matters, how you spend your time matters, the things you do matter, the people you impact matter, the people whose lives you're intertwined with matter, and you matter.

So, regardless of the world doing its dance, making excuses, running way behind schedule, and almost laughing at commitment, obligation, and reality, we need to make sure we don't fall into the trap of complacency. We don't want to fall into that rush of living our lives at breakneck speed, living our lives for things that we have to do, as if we were hamsters on some hamster wheel running round and round who can never get off and keep doing the same thing, frantically, every day but never get anywhere.

Life is a gift. Our bodies are but rentals that we have to return when we are done with them. I just pray that you would truly take time to reflect on what is important, on who you are, on the legacy you will leave to your children and to the world. How do you want to be remembered? How do you want be thought of right now in the life you live?I had an interesting experience when I went to the dentist for some dental work one morning. I went in at 8:00 in the morning and the dental technician, who was taking care of me prior to the dentist coming in to see me, was prowling around in my mouth with a sharp object. It became evident to me that she was drunk, wasted, or hung over from the night before. Obviously, I was extremely annoyed and upset she was there in that condition, much less with a sharp instrument in my mouth. I was about to get up out of the chair and explode at the dentist when God's Holy Spirit told me to stay in the chair and talk to this girl.

I had seen this girl a few years ago. She had worked intermittently at the dentist's office and I think I had given her a CD of a sermon I preached one year. You could see, even through the alcohol haze, she was in despair. She was not happy with her life or with her situation.

Instead of jumping up from the chair and finding the dentist to yell at, I heeded to the Spirit of the Lord and began to talk. I had the opportunity to witness to this girl. What she told me broke my heart. She told me that she and her twin sister used to lay on the bed at night when they were six years old and pray to God to help them from an abusive father and that those prayers were not answered. She told me that later in her life, her father told her he wished they had never been born.

I thought how tragic that was, that any little child should have to suffer that way, that any little child would not know the true love of their mother or father. My heart just broke for this girl. I was just weeping inside as she stumbled around the dentist's office, as I was dodging her with my mouth trying to avoid getting a serious injury while she was still working on me. I realized as I looked at the mess that she was — an emotional and physical mess — I just thought, my Lord, this is why you died on the cross. Jesus, you died for her, you died for me and my job was to share the love of Christ with her and not to admonish her.

So, I attempted to do that, but it was quite difficult. How do you tell a thirty-something girl, whose prayers weren't answered at six years old, who did everything right at six years old, who kneeled at her bedside and prayed to God and didn't get the answer to her prayers that she desired? How do you tell her that God is with her and in her prayers? As I was lying in that dentist's chair, God put on my heart that my job was to come up with a way, to come up with a message through God's word to share in love to this girl and to others like her, who through no fault of their own, have been dealt what we would consider a raw hand in the game of life — whether a physical deformity or emotional disorder, whether it be a financial blow, a relationship blow — of which they did not deserve or had no control over. God just broke my heart and I studied and prayed and came up with the following answer that I would like to share with you in the hopes that it would inspire you, lift you up, and give you hope. Or if you know someone who is in a similar situation as this girl, pass it along. It's the CD I've enclosed called "Three Strikes, You're Out." I pray God will bless you through it.

Jack Levine

December 2006

(EDITOR'S NOTE: You can read "Three Strikes, You're Out" in Jack's *Book Where the Rubber Meets the Road with God*)

YEARGONE – a look back at…

2006

I invite you to take a few moments now to think about your life. How much pressure to perform are you experiencing at home, on the job, to succeed, to make money, to look better, to feel better, to have better relationships, to have more purpose in life, to be better? Are you allowing this pressure to negatively affect the quality of your life in your thoughts, emotions, attitudes and actions? I encourage you to make a conscious choice right now to enjoy each day of your life. Determine what makes you happy, and purpose in your heart to love God with all that you are and to unconditionally love your family and friends (yes, even the difficult ones!). Get alone with God in His word and be filled with His joy. Devote more time to family and doing the things you enjoy. Your life matters to God and those who count on you. Spend each day well.

2008

GAME CHANGING REALIZATIONS

December, 2008

Dear Friends and Family,

It is with great joy and gratitude that we write to you this holiday season. First of all, we have joy for our relationship with Jesus Christ, our God and Savior, who has blessed us in so many ways that it would take the rest of our lives to try and describe. Second, we have gratitude for the lives we live, for the people who are a part of those lives, who bring us such joy and love and make each and every day of our lives so wonderful. Here's the 2008 update:

ECONOMY

I cannot help but notice many of my friends and acquaintances who seem to be getting devoured in this herd mentality that will surely work against them not only in the short term but in the long term as well. As for me, I have had a chance to experience this country's economic fluctuations for the last thirty or so years as an investor and have come to realize one thing — standard investment advice, standard ways to make money, standard philosophies that have been tested by time are all true and are all STILL true today. The only issue seems to be implementing them properly. What do I mean? Well, it seems that when something is overpriced, people cannot seem to get enough of it and will throw any amount of money and caution to the wind to get it because everybody else has it or everybody wants it. (Keeping up with or ahead of the Joneses.)

However, when something is discounted dramatically so that it appears to have lost its value, people don't want any part of it. That logic is insane. The only question that really matters is — what is the true value of that item? For instance, if there was a $2,000 plasma TV with an actual value of $2,000 and someone tried to sell it to you for $6,000, you would laugh. You would say, "I'm not paying $6,000 for that $2,000 TV." However, if that same $2,000 TV was on sale for $400 (an 80% discount), you would probably run so fast to the store to buy it, your head would spin. If you didn't have the money, you would probably borrow it because the value was so great.

Whether you care to admit it or not, that is exactly the situation we have here in America today, both in the real estate market and in the stock market. When things were overpriced, instead of saying, "I'm not paying this amount of money for this, it's overpriced," people bought it and kept buying it thinking it was going to go up forever. They disregarded its value, as a matter of fact, ignored its true value and only looked at what they thought future profits and value would be. Now, when prices have plummeted below actual values, nobody wants to touch anything. This herd mentality always leads to buying at the top and selling at the bottom. In fact, the people who make a lot of money are the people who have the wherewithal and the courage to step in and buy when others are selling and sell when others are buying. Warren Buffet said it pretty famously just a few weeks ago, "We simply attempt to be fearful when others are greedy and to be greedy only when others are fearful."

So, I just send this letter as a wakeup call to you to just evaluate your own life. I'm not telling you to go out and buy real estate, and I'm not telling you to go out and buy stocks. What I am telling you is dollar cost averaging has been a successful formula for a long, long time and any investment expert will tell you that you should continue to make your investments in a methodical, dollar cost averaging way so that when markets are lower, your dollars will buy more.

As an investor today, you should be very excited, not unhappy that stocks are low and decimated, not unhappy that real estate values are low and decimated. That is of course a disaster on a personal level, and no one wants to see that. But the fact is, it is also an opportunity for investors. America is on sale. Companies and properties that you could have never ever afforded to own are 50-75% off their values and, in an essence, a steal to those who have the wherewithal and the courage to step up against the current trend and buck it.

People looking for safety in banks deposits, CDs, and the cover of T-bills will get eaten up by the rising inflation and rising costs. As a matter of fact, by saving your money too conservatively, you actually lose it, and the only way to keep up with inflation is to invest in a regular way and ride out the storms. Nobody is saying there is not a financial hurricane swirling around; there is, but the hurricane will pass. This financial earthquake, financial tornado, financial fire, financial crisis will pass, and if you believe America will be standing and functioning at the end of this crisis, then clearly, you should be investing in America right now and getting the full benefit of the future gains that are to be reaped by making that investment today. So I just want to urge you and encourage you not to be scared, not to get shaken out. The tragedy is that people get scared when things are going down, they get shaken out, and they lose the gains (by not being in stocks or real estate) that are to come in the future.

They think they are going to time the market twice. They think they are going to get out at the top and get back in at the bottom, but it just doesn't work that way. It's hard enough to time the market once, much less time it twice. The key to long-term success is staying with quality investments, and that is how you make money over time. You don't get shaken out; you don't get scared; you don't fold, especially when you are betting on America, the greatest country in the world.

And if this country goes down and if this country fails, its economic system fails, and its currency is worthless, nothing matters anyway. There'll be chaos in the streets, there'll be civil wars, there'll be nothing left and it won't have mattered anyway. But if, as I believe, the country doesn't go down, if it does stand up, if it is strong, and is resilient and does bounce back, and you are not investing on a regular basis in the market, you will probably miss one of the greatest buying opportunities of all time, and you will regret it the rest of your life.

I am not smart enough to tell you if this stock market or real estate market is at the bottom, if it's got more to go, or where it's going to go. I'm just smart enough to tell you that I'm not getting shaken out, and I'm not getting scared when I see America on sale. I'm getting excited about that. From a real estate perspective, I have a very good grasp on the value of properties in South Florida and North Florida (specifically in Hamilton County), at least I believe I do, and I think I have a very good grasp on the value of the some of the corporations that make up my stock portfolio today. So I am investing with confidence, excited that the dollars I invest each month are dollars that are actually purchasing me more of the companies and properties that I believe in. That is called dollar cost averaging and is a successful formula that will certainly make money over time, so don't get shaken out.

Don't join the herd jumping off the cliff mentality. Stand up against the crowd. If our economy was going to break, and our system was going to break, this September, October, or November would have been the time. As a matter of fact, it could have crashed, it could have ended, but it didn't. And all those people, and I mean this with no disrespect, but all those people who are stockpiling food in the mountains somewhere and hoarding bars of gold saying America would crumble, this was as close as you will ever come to having that theory be a success or a reality. And you know what? Your theory failed! America passed the test.

Oh, it's a painful crisis, and the economic effects of Wall Street carelessness and greed and our own carelessness and greed as investors and consumers, whether it was a technology/Nasdaq stock bubble, the housing market bubble, abuse of credit, or other easy ways we thought we could make money, absolutely there is a price to pay for that. Absolutely it's going to be inconvenient and painful, but absolutely it will pass. America has already withstood many tests, as it did on 9/11, as it did in previous crises. It has withstood the test and has risen again, and it's just a great day to be an American — maybe not financially, but certainly from a prideful perspective. So I just urge you to "keep your head about you while all the others are losing theirs," a piece of advice from Winston Churchill that my father has passed on to me since I was a young man, which has served me very, very well over time. Thank you, Dad.

GOD

I was having trouble coming up with this year's letter. I just couldn't get peace about what to write. I still did not have it together when we left for New York last week (December 11) to go to my nephew, Dylan's, Bar Mitzvah. This, by the way, turned out to be one of the greatest Bar Mitzvahs ever, complete with personalized name-printed jerseys, personalized pictures on footballs and basketballs, and a great time of family and fun. Anyway, I didn't understand why I could not get peace about the letter, as I had been trying to write it since Thanksgiving. Then, when we got back from New York yesterday, I realized that the reason I couldn't get peace about the letter prior was that it wasn't ready to be written until now. God has now given me insight about what he would like me to share with you this year.

It started when we got up to New York last week on Thursday, December 11. The Bar Mitzvah was Saturday the 13th. On Friday the day before, my brother Mike called me and asked me if I would like to come up on stage in Temple and cover up the Torah after Dylan had read from his portion of the Torah at the ceremony. This is a great honor in the Jewish religion, and I said to my brother, "I would be honored and privileged to do it, and I am honored that you asked me. I would be honored to do it as long as you don't feel that me being a Christian would offend anyone." Mike assured me no one would be offended (and I knew he loved me so much that he wouldn't care if anyone was).

I still consider myself Jewish. I have always been and always will be Jewish, regardless of the labels anybody wants to put on me. I am a Jewish person who has accepted Jesus Christ as my Lord and Savior. I have added Jesus to my Jewishness. I have not replaced it.

If you asked me one word to define who I am, I would say I am a Christian, and I would define Christian as one who believes in Jesus Christ as Lord and Savior. By far the most important thing in my life is my relationship with Jesus Christ. It brings me the greatest peace, joy, and happiness. It is more important to me than being Jewish, than being white, than being healthy, than being able to see or hear. I think you get the picture.

God saved my life both literally and figuratively when I was thirty-three years old, and today, I am secure in the knowledge that not only are God and his Holy Spirit living inside of me, but I will be with him in heaven for all eternity. I have known Jesus for eighteen years now, and His promise that He will bless us "exceedingly and abundantly more than we can ask or imagine" is a true one. While there have been trials and tribulations along the way, I have taken great joy and comfort in knowing that God has been with me every step of the way, God loves me, and I am his son. I know how much I love my own children; I would have to multiply that by ten million to even start to get a glimpse of how much God loves me (and that's also how much God loves you, too).

So I accepted that honor to cover up the Torah and sure enough the Bar Mitzvah came Saturday night and I was called up on stage. I was awed as I stood looking up at the Torah, realizing the awesomeness of God. As I heard the rabbi, my nephew Dylan and the congregation offer prayers in the temple, prayers from the Old Testament, prayers from Isaiah, from Deuteronomy, from the Psalms, from Genesis, I couldn't help but come to the conclusion that Jewish people worship the same God we Christians do.

They believe in the same God, but they do not yet understand the sacrifice of Jesus Christ and what it meant. That God, in essence, removed the requirements of the Old Testament laws and replaced them by sending His only son Jesus as an atoning sacrifice/payment for all the sins of man. Thus replacing the requirements of the Old Testament law with His grace, mercy and love. Our salvation, our place in heaven, now comes from God, as it was secured for us by Him, paid for by Him with the blood of His son. This salvation, is a gift from God that you can only receive and accept through faith in Jesus Christ. Somehow, it dawned on me — perhaps like the moment when it dawned on Peter that he was to share the Gospel with the Jews — but it just dawned on me at that moment in temple, that it was the same God. Now I always knew it before, at least intellectually, but I don't think the realization of it or the clarity of it ever hit me so hard. I felt overwhelmed with God's presence and in awe of God as I realized how much the Jewish people love and revere God. I share this with you because the night prior to the Bar Mitzvah, my son, Jackson (who is now six years old), and I were driving back alone to the hotel, and somehow the conversation turned to Temple.

He asked me if the people in Temple believed in Jesus, and I had to tell him the truth. I said, "No, they don't." He got all sad and forlorn and said he was horrified that they didn't believe (because he knows the ramifications of non-belief… a life separated from God for all eternity). Then he asked this simple question that could only come out of the innocent mouth of a child. "Why don't they believe Jesus?" And I said to him, "Listen, each person gets to decide on their own what they will and won't believe." I went on to stress how much we love our family and how our job is to pray for them and all the people who don't know Jesus and also that we are to be examples of what it means to know Jesus Christ and that our life of knowing Christ should reflect something they don't have and something they want. First and foremost it should reflect the peace, joy, mercy and love of Jesus Christ. God says he gives us His peace "which transcends all understanding." I told Jackson I've tried hard to do this over the years, to be a good witness for Christ and that I, as I urged him to do, will continue praying for our family and friends to come to know Christ.

Knowing Jackson has tendency to speak up about what is on his mind (can you say, "Like father, like son!" smile!) I specifically asked Jackson after our talk, "Jackson, please wait until after the Bar Mitzvah to ask anyone why they don't believe in Jesus because it's a very special time for everyone in Temple and we don't want to upset them in any way on this special day of honor… But if you want to ask people after the Bar Mitzvah on Sunday, you can."

So, were riding to Temple in the rental car on Saturday and Jackson was with me, along with my wife, Beth, my oldest son, Ricky (now twenty years old), my daughter, Talia (four years old), and my parents, who are Jewish (Marcia and Jerry). Jackson blurts out to my parents, "Grandma, do you know the people in Temple don't believe in Jesus?" And my mother responds, "Yes, honey, I know. And no, they don't believe in Jesus. But you know what? They believe in God and we are all worshipping the same God." And I let the comment go thinking that, you know what, I really need to address this. It's not the same God; it's different; and while it's a nice convenient answer for my mother to give, I can't let Jackson go to bed thinking it is okay to worship other gods besides Jesus. That was my thought prior to the Bar Mitzvah service.

Then when I was in Temple during the service on stage, looking at the Torah and feeling God impressing the scriptures on my heart, those being read from Genesis, Isaiah, Deuteronomy and Psalms, I realized that it is the same God. It is absolutely the same God and the only thing missing is that they don't understand that the Messiah, who is indeed Jesus, has come. They are still searching for the Messiah. But, as I stood there, there was no doubt in my mind that the same God who raised Jesus Christ from the dead was the same God who talked to Israel and the Jewish people. It's not a different God. It's not separate. It's the same God, and my prayer today for every one of my Jewish friends and every friend who does not know Jesus Christ personally, as Lord and Savior, is that they accept the greatest gift God has ever given — the gift of Jesus Christ, so they, too, may know him for all eternity.

God is God. Not me. God is God, and He offers this gift to everyone — Jews and Gentiles alike — so that all may come to know him and all may have the benefit of abundant life and life eternal. It's ironic in today's economy, where we have watched our government change the rules of the game whether it is a ban on short-selling, the increase of FDIC insured bank deposits from $100,000 to $250,000, a bail out of brokerage firms, auto dealers, or the economy in general. There is a lot of unprecedented action, a lot of "breaking the rules." All in all, I've heard people say the same thing, "They changed the rules; they changed the rules! The game is different, the game is different!" (YES, THEY DID CHANGE THE RULES. THEY HAD TO OR THE GAME WOULD HAVE BEEN OVER AND IT WOULD HAVE ENDED IN DEATH FOR OUR ECONOMY.)

We also need to understand that God changed the rules. (YES, GOD CHANGED THE RULES AND HE HAD TO OR IT WOULD HAVE ENDED IN DEATH FOR YOU AND ME. BUT, GOD LOVED US SO MUCH HE CHANGED THE RULES SO WE COULD LIVE WITH HIM FOREVER!)

When God sacrificed his son Jesus on the cross, He changed the rules for our benefit, for our blessing, so that we wouldn't be separated from Him. We would finally be with Him, without separation and have that unique, one-on-one individual relationship with God himself that is now available because Jesus paid the price for our sins. We deserve to die for our sins, but Jesus paid the price so that we can live with Him and be with Him forever. God did that! The God of Israel did that! The God who created the world, the God of the book of Genesis, the God who said, "In the beginning, there was light!" did that! That same God is the God who gave us Jesus. I pray that the scales will be removed from the eyes of nonbelievers, so that people will see, that their ears will be open, and that their hearts will soften and receive this great gift from God this Christmas season. I pray that no one will miss the amazing blessings of eternal life and an abundant life (living with and walking with God) that God has in store for every believer.

Jackson was horrified at the realization that people in Temple weren't going to be in Heaven (John 3:16 "For God so loved the world that he gave his one and only son …that whoever believes in him shall have eternal life") and that's what got him so upset because he loves people so much. But Jackson and I have talked again and he understands the difference. He understands he is to love all people with the love of Christ and I am certain he understands how fortunate and blessed he is to have Jesus in his life. How lucky and wonderful are children who grow up knowing God…they are so blessed, and next to my own relationship with Jesus Christ, my kids knowing God is the best gift God could ever have given me (or any other parent) — to see their children walking with The Lord and growing in their personal relationship with God.

I also had a regret when I was in Temple, when I realized that it was the same God. I regretted not going to Hebrew school. I regretted not knowing God when I grew up, but I thank God for his mercy. I thank God for the last eighteen years since I've known Jesus. I know more now about the Bible and the Old Testament probably than I would have ever learned in Hebrew school, so I'm grateful that God saw fit to restore this knowledge to me in this way.

GOD WORKING IN MY LIFE

Recently, God has brought a brother into my life to bring me closer to God by stretching my faith and growing me even more in my personal walk with God. My wife is friends with another mom at Jackson and Talia's school (Glades Christian Academy). Beth mentioned to me a few weeks ago her friend, has a brother, David, who is a full-time missionary and his mission is primarily to homeless people. He travels from his home in Central New York to Toronto to Times Square in new York City and Rochester and other cities ministering the love of Christ to the homeless, to the most hopeless, lost and desperate people you have ever seen. She forwarded us an e-mail he had sent her that was very inspiring to me and really touched my heart. Beth then mentioned David was coming into town to visit Heidi and asked if I would like to meet him. I said, "Yeah! I would really like that!" This is really strange for me because, by nature, I am a recluse at heart and I just don't go out of my way to meet new people (especially at my house! smile!) But, I sensed I was supposed to meet this guy.

In the short hour and a half that we spent together, Beth, Ricky and I had the privilege of hearing David share his testimony about how he had sold out completely to God. He had sold his landscaping business nine years ago and followed God's call to minister to homeless people. He had gotten rid of all his possessions and lives on God's provisions, sleeps in hostels and YMCAs and on the road, basically lives like the Apostle Paul did, going from place to place with nothing but the word of God. He felt so called and led by Christ to share God's word that he literally sold all of the things and possessions he had accumulated on Earth and traded his life as a sacrificial love offering to Jesus, and for that I know he will receive additional treasures in the Kingdom of Heaven. I so admire his sacrifice and dedication and the fact that he actually did it. Everybody talks about it but nobody is willing to do it. Everybody talks about how much they love Jesus, but most are not willing to show it with all of their lives. Maybe we give an hour a week in church and some other limited form of service at our convenience (and I include myself in this group of people).

Most of us are not willing to live and walk as Jesus did, and here I met this guy, who had actually sold everything for Christ. I couldn't help to feel somewhat envious of him; this guy is sold out 100% and I'm not. Maybe I'm sold out to Christ 60%, maybe 80% but not 100%, and I need to examine myself. I believe God brought this brother into my life for this specific purpose at this specific time in my life to draw me closer to God, so I can gain a deeper understanding of my relationship with God and so, with that deeper understanding in place, God could bless me even more and show me greater things as He (my Father God) draws me closer to Him.

This doesn't mean that every one of us are supposed to be missionaries and are supposed to live our lives ministering to homeless people, but it does mean as God said that we are to be 100% sold out for Jesus Christ. Our lives are to count for the kingdom of God. We are to be the bride of Christ and focus our attention on Him — not on the treasures of this world that will rot, rust and decay, but on Jesus Christ himself.

> *"Do not store up for yourselves treasures on Earth, where moths and rust destroy, and where thieves break in and steal. But store up for yourselves treasures in heaven, where moths and rust do not destroy, and where thieves do not break in and steal. For where your treasure is, there your heart will be also." (Matthew 6:19-21)*

I just thank God that he brought David into my life to open my eyes and I know that God uses people, circumstances and events to bring us closer to Him. I trust and pray that you will look in your own life for the people, circumstances and events that God puts into your life to bring you closer to Him. Don't ignore them, but find them and embrace them.

David is not God. He's not a perfect human being, but he is one of the few people I've met in my life who have totally, 100% sold out to Jesus Christ. I have known that those people who have forsaken all of this world for Jesus Christ's sake… their reward in Heaven (for those who follow Christ completely and totally like David) will be tremendous. That is the reward I want. It's the pat on the back I want when I get to Heaven and see Jesus. I want Him to look at me, smile and say, "Well done, good and faithful servant." I want to know that I followed Jesus' instructions; I did what He told me. I sold out for Christ. I didn't get sucked up in the things of this world, the things that were so meaningless. Instead, I focused on what matters — God and His kingdom — and I invested my life in the kingdom of God. There lies the greatest reward for all Christians… in that simple act of total faith and obedience to the will of God. I'll say it again….Therein lays the greatest reward for all Christians! Not only in Heaven, but as we live that life now. That's what gives me joy, pleasure, and happiness — when I'm focused on Christ. I find that when I am focused on the world, I only get anxious, depressed, upset, irritated, annoyed, agitated, unhappy, and a lot of other adjectives that you can fill in for yourself. When I'm focused on God, which is where I need to be, and when I walk in the shadow of the Lord, I am joyful, peaceful and happy. I can do all things through Him who lives in me.

BRUCE SPRINGSTEEN AND DEATH

After all the amazing live Bruce shows we had in 2008, we are now looking forward to a new round of Bruce Springsteen tours in 2009. I won't bore you with the details again of how much pleasure I get from these shows, but I will share with you that in this past year, 2008, Bruce was touring and unfortunately, his long-time keyboard player, Danny Federici, passed away from melanoma Cancer in April in the middle of the tour… I had the privilege of seeing the first three shows Bruce played soon after Danny died. I have to tell you those were probably the three greatest Bruce Springsteen shows I've ever seen in my life. It's hard to believe, since I've seen so many (at least 150). It starts back in 1975 but nonetheless, they were the best and I want to share with you why.

It seemed that Danny's death got Bruce thinking about his own mortality and, as such, what had become a polished show, still great, but certainly polished and tight was now abandoned and all caution was thrown to the wind. What we saw in those shows after Danny died, which by the way continued until the tour ended in September, was a newfound passion for life, a newfound passion for music, a newfound passion for the audience. Perhaps Bruce realized that his time on Earth was limited too and he didn't know how many good years he had left.

He also realized that things don't stay the same forever. Here was a band that had been together for over thirty years and probably thought they would be together forever, and now life and God was changing their plans and their reality. I think Bruce realized this and took it to a new level — a level filled with spontaneity, with audibles from the crowd, taking obscure and not so obscure requests, not knowing what was going to come next. This truly allowed for what Springsteen fans across the world would say were some of the best concerts we have ever seen in our lives, dating back to that 1973-1981 time when what we saw was beyond description… when the raw, fresh energy and excitement and life commentary and dreams of our future came alive in music and rock-n-roll exploded at once, all through Springsteen's lyrics, music, and concerts, which sometimes lasted for six hours.

In the last twenty years we have all grown up and accepted the fact that Bruce was older too. Concerts now lasted a mere two and a half or three hours, but we took what we could get. Nothing ever mirrored those early days… until now. Until Danny died and Bruce let go of the ordinary, he let go of the schedule, he let go of the set list. He really let go of the rigidity, which had come to mark probably his music and his life in the last twenty years, and went back to being young again.

I say that for all of us as an example, and I say that we all need to let go of the rigidity and the scheduling and the forced actions that make up our lives and seem to be what we call living. I call it existing... but that's not living. If your existence is not bringing you true joy and happiness, you are just wasting your own time and, to the best of your ability, you should make sure you are seeking true joy and happiness and finding it. It's not too late to start to live your life, rather than just existing.

I've obviously found "living" in my relationship with Jesus Christ, and I recommend that you do the same. But I parallel back to Bruce. You could see him laughing, smiling, happy, joyful, and spontaneous again — living life to the fullest again. We all felt it. Every one of us in the audience at each of the shows felt it and just rode along. It was a great wave and it just made me realize that we all need to grow young again; we all need to throw off the crap that hinders our joy. That we need to throw off our to-do list, our schedules, our rigidity, the things that we do, that we live by, and unleash our inner selves and unlock that cage that holds us prisoner to the world and its expectations. As a result of that freedom, live a life that's full of joy and spontaneity and happiness. Now, that doesn't mean quit your job, get on a plane, blow your savings, and go to Hawaii, but within reason. Live, man... LIVE! Look inside your heart, inside your soul. Let loose, break free, break out, into the person God made you to be. Live life to the fullest each and every day, based on your personal definition.

So this Holiday season, I ask you to re-examine your own life and say, "In this past year, have I accomplished the things I wanted to accomplish?" And if not, say, "What am I going to do to accomplish this next year because I don't want to let more time go by that seems to be wasted time when I look back."

One last lesson we learned on our trip to New York last week, and perhaps the most important; while we were up there freezing our butts off for four days, we learned that we should never, ever, ever, ever, EVER, take living in Florida for granted. We just love Florida so much and I just thank God for bringing me to Florida in 1985, bringing me where I needed to be, and I hope that this holiday season, I pray this holiday season, that God will bring you spiritually and physically where you need to be, which is always to a closer walk with God.

As usual we've enclosed a few CD's sermons I had the privilege of preaching that I thought you would enjoy, and we pray that God blesses you and speaks directly to your heart through it. God Bless you and your family this holiday season and always! Have a great 2009.

Love,

Jack and Beth, Ricky, Jackson & Talia

P.S. Following are some scriptures we wanted to share with you this holiday season.

> *He who dwells in the shelter of the Most High*
> *will rest in the shadow of the Almighty.*
>
> *I will say of the Lord, "He is my refuge and my fortress,*
> *my God, in whom I trust."*
>
> *(Psalm 91:1-2)-*

Great is our Lord and mighty in power;
* his understanding has no limit.*

The Lord sustains the humble
* but casts the wicked to the ground.*

The Lord delights in those who fear him,
* who put their hope in his unfailing love.*

(Psalm 147:5-6, 11)

Oh, that their hearts would be inclined to fear me and keep all my commands always, so that it might go well with them and their children forever!

So be careful to do what the Lord your God has commanded you; do not turn aside to the right or to the left. Walk in all the way that the Lord your God has commanded you, so that you may live and prosper and prolong your days in the land that you will possess.

(Deuteronomy 5:29 & 32, 33)

Hear, O Israel: The Lord our God, the Lord is one. Love the Lord your God with all your heart and with all your soul and with all your strength.

(Deuteronomy 6:4-5)

In the beginning God created the heavens and the Earth.

And God said, "Let there be light."

Then God said, "Let us make man in our image, in our likeness, and let them rule over the fish of the sea and the birds of the air, over the livestock, over all the Earth, and over all the creatures that move along the ground."

So God created man in his own image, in the image of God he created him; male and female he created them.

(Genesis 1:1, 3, 26-27)

Give ear and come to me;
    hear me, that your soul may live.
    I will make an everlasting covenant with you,
    my faithful love promised to David.

Seek the Lord while he may be found;
    call on him while he is near.

Let the wicked forsake his way
    and the evil man his thoughts.
    Let him turn to the Lord, and he will have mercy on him,
    and to our God, for he will freely pardon.

"For my thoughts are not your thoughts,
    neither are your ways my ways,"
    declares the Lord.

"As the heavens are higher than the Earth,
    so are my ways higher than your ways

(Isaiah 55:3, 6-9)

"This is the covenant I will make with the house of Israel
  after that time," declares the Lord.
  "I will put my law in their minds
  and write it on their hearts.
  I will be their God,

No longer will a man teach his neighbor,
  or a man his brother, saying, 'Know the Lord,'
  because they will all know me,
  from the least of them to the greatest,"
  declares the Lord.
  "For I will forgive their wickedness
  and will remember their sins no more."

(Jeremiah 31:33-34)

For I know the plans I have for you," declares the Lord,

"plans to prosper you and not to harm you,

plans to give you hope and a future.

Then you will call upon me and come and pray to me, and I will listen to you

You will seek me and find me when you seek me with all your heart."

(Jeremiah 29: 11-13)

YEARGONE – a look back at…

2008

How about you? Have you ever stopped for a moment to consider your own mortality like Bruce Springsteen did when his long-time keyboard player, Danny Federici, passed away? Life on this earth is short whether you live 70, 80, 90 or 100 years. The time passes very quickly. I challenge you to evaluate your life. Make sure you are making it count for the Kingdom of God. Let go of the ordinary, the rigidity, the complacency, and LIVE full of joy, happiness and freedom for God. Believe me, God wants you to THRIVE not simply survive. Do something spontaneous in love today. Take your wife for a special date; take your children for an unplanned ice cream, or swimming, camping, roller skating or to a ballgame or picnic. Live instead of existing. You will be glad you did! God loves you so much!

2009

LEAVE A LEGACY

December, 2009

HOLIDAY LETTER

Happy holiday, everybody. Merry Christmas. Happy Hanukah and Happy New Year to all of our friends and family. It's such a joy to be able to write again this holiday season. Another wonderful year has gone by and we look forward to and thank God for His gift to us of Life and each day of the year to come. Here's the 2009 update:

LIFE

I'm reminded this holiday season of just how much we have to be grateful for. I spoke to a guy named Brad on the phone yesterday for the first time, a radio promotion guy in Chicago whose online bio stated he had multiple sclerosis. I asked him how he handled MS and its crippling effects (he's in a wheel chair permanently). He was telling me how it pained him so much to see his caregivers getting to tickle his young sons and how desperately he wanted to be able to do it himself, but he knew he never could. And how he so wished he did not have the physical infirmities of MS and was not confined to the wheelchair so he could play baseball and football with his sons, but he knew he would never again be able to do that.

It made me realize how we take for granted the little things that are truly the most important things, that God has given us; the ability to walk, to eat, to taste, to breathe, to love, to live, and to laugh. Those of us who are able to do these things with no limitations should be so very grateful each and every day. We truly should be leaping and rejoicing. I guess we don't really realize what we have until it's gone and we take so much of it for granted. Hearing the regret in his voice made me even more determined not to take for granted the gifts God has already given me. I felt stupid for focusing so intently on selfish things such as finances, the future, and other worries and cares that were interrupting and eliminating the joy I should be feeling and living today, as we realize just how much we already really have! (I'm not saying don't think about these things I'm just saying that our happiness and joy should not be dependent upon those things and those outcomes. They should be dependent on and because of our relationship with God.) So my holiday prayer for each and every one of you is that today you will be joyful and count your blessings and not your tears. (And if you're not sure, just take a quick trip to Haiti and see the people living in poverty — that's real poverty not the U.S. kind — or a quick visit to a local children's hospital will both change your perspective on life real quick.)

I MEET THE BOSS

I met Bruce Springsteen this year, spent more than a half hour with him after his show in Fort Lauderdale. For those of you who have known me for years, you know I'm a big fan of his music and what a treat that was for me. Just as I hoped and imagined he would be, Bruce was a great guy, very personable, very down to Earth. Maybe it's because of listening to his music all these years, but I felt like I had known him all my life. It was everything I hoped it would be and just a wonderful memory I will cherish. We talked about family, our kids, baseball, the Yankees, the band, life, getting older, celebrity status, preaching, what it's like for him to come down after being on such a three-hour high. And there were a lot of special insights dating back to the recording of the "Born to Run" album through the intensity and insanity of the current tour. It was a great time, Andy Brief (my longtime New York advertising friend) and I got to meet Bruce alone in his dressing room back stage and I got to go to some great Bruce concerts this year, in Fort Lauderdale, Tampa, New York, Atlanta and Washington with Andy Brief and my brother Mike and I making the rounds. Just for the record, as much as I love Bruce shows, I'd rather spend time talking about God than meeting Bruce or going to a Bruce show… but hey, you take what you can get!

THE ECONOMY

I know that the economy has continued to be crippling despite what you read in the newspapers. I am hearing and seeing things are still very bad. People are still without work, things cost more and people who are working make less. That's just the bottom line. Continue to be in prayer for our country's leaders and the health and future of our country. I hope that when you got my letter last year, you took note of my suggestion that we do not get shaken out of the stock market but continue to dollar cost average in. If you had done so as of the writing of this letter you would be up over 35% had you simply held on to your position from last December and continued dollar cost averaging.

I'm not claiming to be a stock sage or sear. I had no crystal ball, just a firm belief in this country and smart investing principles that have been time tested. That doesn't mean that the stock market will continue to go up this year, but it does mean that I still believe in the same principles and values that I shared with you last year. One of them is you don't get shaken out when everybody is selling. You invest in things that have value and you continue to invest in them if you believe in them. On that note I would think that the thing with the most value to you is your life, and I would really question you this holiday season to ask yourself where and what are you investing your life in.

Are you investing your life in material things that will disappear, that will rust and decay? We replaced an old big screen TV recently that had basically been reduced to a pile of junk by new technology and wear and tear. Yet I remember how proud and excited I was the day in 1992 when I got that new TV. Now it had become a worthless piece of junk. Just like every new car, every new item of clothing, every new toy, at some point they're all given away, thrown away, or useless.

That's God's reminder to us this holiday season. The things of the world should not be our treasure. Our treasure should be our relationship with God. That our joy should come from our relationship with God, and that's something we can have for free. It's God's gift to us and He wants us to have it.

So I just want to remind you this holiday season to ask yourself what you are investing your life in. If you're already investing your life in God, I would remind you to invest more of it in God. The more you invest in God, the more return you will get. Gods says it in Mark chapter 4, verse 20 in the Bible, "And the seed that fell on good soil represents those who hear and accept God's word and produce a harvest of thirty, sixty, or even a hundred times as much as had been planted!" Another translation (the Message Bible) puts it this way, "But the seed planted in the good earth represents those who hear the Word, embrace it, and produce a harvest beyond their wildest dreams."

So I hope this holiday season you would do something very special. It would be a gift to yourself and to your family regardless of when you chose to give it to them, whether it's now, a year from now, or perhaps you leave it for when you go home to meet the Lord Jesus Christ for others to read. I just pray that you would write a journal, make notes, and use this letter as your motivation and starting point for your family journal. I have enclosed a few questions that you can answer to get you started. Perhaps you can capture some of the thoughts and moments in your life that would be most important and most critical to you. Plus they will definitely make you think! Hopefully then you can share them with your family and friends at the appropriate time. It does matter. And it's a shame if people don't know what you are really thinking and how you really feel.

I hope you would take this to heart and use this opportunity to share some of your feelings and thoughts with yourself. Hopefully then you can share them with your family and friends at the appropriate time. It does matter. And it's a shame if people don't know what you are really thinking and how you really feel.

We get so busy in our lives, living and doing stuff, and we forget to tell the people we love how important they are to us. We forget to share the things that we've learned and the wisdom that we have with other people who can benefit from it and be blessed by it so greatly. Then the time comes, as I said in the beginning of this letter, like the guy Brad from Chicago, where either physically (like him with MS or friends and family that we're losing to cancer and other diseases, old age included) or mentally, capacities diminish, circumstances change, life-changing events occur and all of the sudden you are either no longer in the mood, have the desire, or the capability to share the wisdom and things you have learned with others. Oh what a blessing it would be for others to benefit from that wisdom and insight. So please, this Holiday season, give this gift to yourself. I promise you will have so much fun. You'll laugh, you'll cry, you'll be happy, you'll be sad, but you'll run the gamut of emotions as you answer these questions and fill out your journal. They will really get you thinking about your life, and I hope you will be excited not only about the things you have written, but more importantly, I hope you realize there are blank pages to be written on in the years ahead.

CLOSING THOUGHTS ON LIFE!

The role you play in your job, your money, your position, where you live, what you look like, doesn't define who you are in life. What defines you is who you are inside. If that's the case, you can play any role in life and be comfortable with it. You can be and do anything because these things don't define who you are. It's who you are inside that defines you. Not what you do!

The problem most people have is that they let the roles of their life define who they are. They let their job, their marriage, their money, their health, their looks, and other people's opinions of them — good or bad — define who they are. But that's not the definition of who we are. The definition of who we are is God's kids. God created us and we should be rejoicing in that fact — rejoicing in our inheritance in the kingdom of God, rejoicing in our treasures and in keys to the kingdom that God has given us and our relationship with God. We shouldn't need anything else to define who we are, and certainly God doesn't use anything else to define who we are.

Well I think that's it for now…

All our love from sunny Florida,

Jack and Beth, Ricky, Jackson & Talia

JOURNAL QUESTIONS

Now remember, this is your private journal, you can use as much paper as you want to answer these questions. You can dictate your answers onto a tape recorder or type them on your computer or just hand write them on a pieces of paper. I've numbered the questions so you don't have to write them out again. Just write the question number down and start answering it.

Remember, these are just suggestions to get you going…you can add and answer any other questions or thoughts or topics you think of or want to talk about…so have fun… (and tell the truth). After all it's your life we are talking about! You don't have to answer all the questions at once. You can do one a day, a few a day, or even a few a week if you want. You'll be amazed at how soon you are done with these and off writing about current things in your life. Then your very own journal will be up to date and accurate… and YOU'LL BE ON THE WAY TO WRITING YOUR FIRST BOOK (smile!).

1. What was the happiest time of your life?
2. What was the saddest time of your life?
3. Who influenced you the most and how did they do it?
4. What was the best advice you ever got? Who did it come from?
5. If you could give advice to anyone, what advice would you give to someone just graduating college?
6. If you could give advice to anyone, what advice would you give to someone just getting married?
7. If you could give advice to anyone, what advice would you give to someone just starting in business?

8. What do you believe is the most important thing a person can do in their life?
9. How would like to be remembered by those who know and love when you die?
10. If there was something you could change about your life, what would that be?
11. What is your biggest regret in life?
12. What is your most cherished childhood memory?
13. What is your most cherished adult memory?
14. What is your fondest memory of each of your children?
15. What is your fondest memory of your parents?
16. What is your fondest memory of your wife/husband?
17. What is your fondest memory of your best friend?
18. Who have you met in your life that you would say is truly remarkable and why?
19. What is your favorite thing to do?
20. What makes you the happiest?
21. If you could have dinner with any three people who have been a part of your life (regardless of how long you knew them) who would those people be and why?
22. Who was the best teacher you ever had and why?
23. If money wasn't an object and you could have done anything you wanted to with your life… looking back what would you have done?
24. What is your greatest passion in life?

26. What was your favorite kind of music?

27. What was your favorite band? Why?

28. What was your favorite song? Why?

29. What was your favorite movie of all time and why?

30. Was there a certain turning point or turning points in your life when your life changed dramatically? List up to three. Where and when did they happen?

31. From these turning-point events, what changed in your life — either for better or worse — as a result of them?

32. What do you wish you could do more with the people you know and love?

33. What is your view on politics?

34. Who is the best president we ever had during your life and why?

35. Do you think the country is in worse shape now or better shape than when you were a kid and why?

35. What was the funniest thing you ever did as a child? As an adult?

36. What is the funniest thing each of your children has done?

37. What is the funniest movie you ever watched? Why?

NOW GET CREATIVE AND MAKE UP YOUR OWN QUESTIONS TO ANSWER, OR SHARE YOUR OWN PERSONAL INSIGHTS ON ANYTHING OR ANY SUBJECT YOU WANT TO (and even those you don't want to!)

YEARGONE – a look back at…

2009

2009 reminded me we have so much for which to be thankful. Who and what are you thankful for today? Purpose in your heart not to take the little things in life such as breath and the ability to walk, talk and laugh for granted. Give thanks for your true treasure: relationship with God and loved ones. I encourage you to begin your journal today using the questions in this year's chapter to help you get started. This process will capture your most important thoughts, emotions and special memories. Others need the benefit of your wisdom and insight. You are valuable!

2010

SHORT TERM PAIN, LONG TERM GAIN

December, 2010

Happy Holidays and Merry Christmas!

To our wonderful family and friends...We want you to know that we truly consider it an honor, joy and privilege to have you as part of our lives. Each and every one of you has been a tremendous blessing to our lives, and you are often in our thoughts and prayers. We pray that God blesses you abundantly and exceedingly more than you can ask or imagine, that your walk with God is a joyful and peaceful one, and that you make the most of this wonderful gift of life we have been given.

There is so much going on this holiday season! I want to share with you some thoughts from my heart, which I hope will impact you in a positive way as you look forward into the New Year and reflect on the year that has passed.

First, there was my hernia, a physical issue I was dealing with. For two years prior, the hernia had been diagnosed as a groin tear by a couple of top surgeons and had not yet become a hernia, so I suffered from its effects as a groin tear for two years. It greatly restricted my ability to play baseball and my ability to lift my kids — two of my favorite pastimes. Good news! I had surgery to fix it on December 7 and am on the mend already.

I was actually happy to hear that, indeed, the groin tear had become a hernia and that they would be able operate. I was happy because there was finally a light at the end of the tunnel. It was able to be fixed. I had already accepted the fact of living with a groin tear for the rest of my life, so to know it could be fixed made me feel like I had won the lottery. While I was not looking forward to the short-term pain of surgery and recovery, I was excited and delighted at the prospect that the problem would finally disappear. So, I anticipated the hernia surgery with excitement. I was happy about it, glad that it was coming. I even anticipated the recovery period with joy because I knew it was short term, not permanent. I knew that there was an end to the pain in sight.

God has laid on my heart to share with you that we are to look at our lives here on Earth the same way. God has made this magnificent promise to us, *"And the God of all grace, who called you to his eternal glory in Christ, after you have suffered a little while, will himself restore you and make you strong, firm and steadfast." (1 Peter 5:10)* If we believe something is short term, something like pain and suffering, we can put up with it… especially if we believe it's for our long-term benefit. Obviously childbirth is a classic example and, for me, this hernia was an example of the same concept.

This life we live on Earth is a short-term deal and with the love of God in our hearts, we should be able to be joyful and peaceful through all the circumstances, through any challenges we face. If you are Christian (and many of our friends and family are), you know our place in heaven with God is assured when our time on Earth is over. So we are to remember to be God's examples here on Earth — His proof, His ambassadors, His soldiers, His children, demonstrating and reflecting the love and characteristics of God to a world full of darkness, a world without hope. We are to be the hope and light of God. I hope and pray that you will see your life (as God has shown me mine) in those exact terms.

It was so clear to me through the hernia surgery as it was easy to live with the short-term pain, knowing that just around the corner was a pain-free life, a return back to the normal life I desired. So, our life on this Earth is the same way, especially from God's perspective... which should be our perspective. See what the Word of God says:

> *"In all this you greatly rejoice, though now for a little while you may have had to suffer grief in all kinds of trials. These have come so that the proven genuineness of your faith—of greater worth than gold, which perishes even though refined by fire—may result in praise, glory and honor when Jesus Christ is revealed." (1 Peter 1:6-7)*

> *"Consider it pure joy, my brothers and sisters, whenever you face trials of many kinds, because you know that the testing of your faith produces perseverance. Let perseverance finish its work so that you may be mature and complete, not lacking anything." (James 1:2-4)*

> *"No temptation has overtaken you except what is common to mankind. And God is faithful; he will not let you be tempted beyond what you can bear. But when you are tempted, he will also provide a way out so that you can endure it." (I Corinthians 10:13)*

For those of you, family and friends, who are not Christians, I hope that you will see through the behavior of Christian believers the great joy and peace we have comes from God, our love for Him, trust in Him and gratitude for all He has done for us. I hope that I, my family, and other Christians demonstrate that we do trust God, that we believe in heaven and we believe God's word is true. That belief and certainty (often called "faith") is what enables us to live such joyful, peaceful, happy lives even as we too experience the same trials, tragedies and suffering as everybody else in the world. But, we know that Earth is not our permanent residence and that death is just the beginning of an eternal life with God.

We shouldn't fear death. Obviously we don't want to die and be away from our friends and family. We want to be able to raise our kids and be a part of their lives. We want to love everybody here on Earth for a very long time. But we know what the afterlife holds. We know where we are going. We know that after our life on Earth is done, we will be with God forever in heaven. We know that death is just the beginning for us, the beginning of an eternity with God. I think that's the defining difference in the Christian life.

I think philosopher Blaise Pascal said it best to non-Christians in what is known as "Pascal's Wager." Pascal simply stated that you are better off choosing to believe in God, for if God is real, you get all the benefits of it here and forever in eternity. If God is not real, you still get all the benefits of believing during this life (living worry free without fear of death). Obviously, Christians believe that God is real. If you don't, I strongly recommend you consider the logic and merit of Pascal's Wager… as it's the best bet you could ever make. Google it for yourself, if you dare!

I'm reminded this holiday season of a buddy of mine who was going through some marital issues with his new bride. As I and another friend were giving him the benefit of our years of married experience, he told us his wife told him that she missed "us," meaning that she missed the time that the two of them spent together when they were dating and madly in love. God prompted my heart and I was reminded that God probably feels the same way about many of us. I wonder if God is saying to us this holiday season "He misses US." He misses spending time with us and feeling like He is a priority in our life. My advice to my friend was that he should start spending quality time with his wife and letting her know that he missed "us," too. My friend had to make a conscious effort to rekindle the feelings of being "madly in love" with his wife, like at the beginning of their relationship. I urge you this holiday season to make a conscious effort to rekindle your relationship with God. Imagine God is sitting up in heaven saying He misses you, He misses your time together, and He misses spending time with you. RIGHT NOW is the time to clarify your priorities for the holiday season… first and foremost, put God first! From Him come all blessings and all things good.

This holiday season, I reflected on the recent loss of some dear friends and family, as well as some of my parents' friends, who I had known all my life, who also passed away this year. To me, the only difference was how people faced the end of their lives. Some were afraid, confused, lonely and scared, and their families reacted the same way. Others, who knew and had that relationship with Christ were embracing the life they lived, grateful for the time they had, thanking God for His wonder, grace, and glory, and the certainty that someday they would see their loved ones again.

To me the true tragedy is missing out on the gift of God for your life, on the relationship with God, on the certainty of the afterlife in heaven that God has promised. It was driven home to me this year through all the loss; I hope and pray that you have peace with that issue. I also pray that you will not be one who is worried, scared, upset, aggravated or frustrated at the thought of this life ending, but instead will be one who is grateful to God for any time He has given us, whatever that time may be.

I want to tell you about the true agony I saw in one friend who died this year. He was such a great guy; I've known him for many years. He had a falling out with his son quite a few years ago, and they haven't spoken in many years. You could tell he regretted their riff and separation. He did try to patch things up but was turned down; thus, he was unable to accomplish repairing that relationship. As intelligent, kind, loving, wonderful and sweet of a man as he was since I've known him, it was easy to see he was sorry for the things he had done in the past that had adversely affected his family. The tragic part was that his son never forgave him. Now I don't know what happened; I wasn't there. I'm not judging who was right or wrong in the situation. Regardless of who was at fault, the end result was the same... it was a tragedy. This guy was sincerely sorry for what he had done; he wanted to rekindle that relationship but was unable to do so. For as long as I knew him, it was a great regret; he died still having that regret. Fortunately, he had a relationship with the Lord. He is now in heaven with Jesus and no longer suffers regrets about anything, and we thank God for that.

Sadly, we see this situation all too often these days with family members and friends. I sincerely ask you to look into your own life this holiday season and see if there is anybody you haven't forgiven. Think about how much those people would appreciate and be blessed by your forgiveness. Imagine the love they would receive from your forgiveness, given freely as God has given us His unconditional love and forgiveness. I pray that God will bless your heart with the gift of forgiveness for anyone you believe has wronged you, whether family or friend, anyone who may have done something to offend you. Life is too short; you can see it when people aren't here anymore, but then it's too late to make amends. I pray you seek God's counsel regarding making your amends.

This year we also said goodbye to my friend Sandy Mazer, a great guy and true friend for twenty-five years, who died suddenly leaving behind a faithful, loving wife and two children. I am delighted to say Sandy came to know Jesus Christ in the last few years of his life and is at home with the Lord. I was so inspired and impressed by his wife Denise, a Christian believer, who just responded so lovingly and faithfully to God. She was so grateful for the life that they had... not bitter at life's circumstances but better because of her solid faith in God. She trusted God with all things in her life, especially those that mattered most to her — her family. What a great witness and testimony to a sold-out Christian life.

One of my old college roommates also passed away this year. I haven't seen or spoken to him in thirty years. He was one of the most intelligent guys I ever met, but he smoked cigarettes all his life and died of lung cancer. So I guess he wasn't very smart in that regard. We lost touch after college; I think he purposely isolated himself from everyone. I always viewed his life as a great tragedy. He felt the world had dealt him a bad hand, (his parents divorced early, etc.) but he could have easily overcome it. He was that smart. Instead he chose to live as a victim, seeking relief from his own mind and life by isolating himself and numbing himself with a variety of other vices. So how are you living? As a victim? Or as the son of God, the King's kid, heir to the throne of heaven along with Jesus? The choice is yours. Bob Dylan said it best, "You either have faith or you have unbelief, but there's no neutral ground."

It's a privilege and a pleasure to be able to use the gifts God has given me — the ability to communicate verbally and in writing the thoughts in my head. God has wired me that way and I want to make sure I use that gift for the glory and kingdom of God. Each of us is wired with different gifts from God, and we are to make sure we use those gifts to serve Him, to serve each other, and to declare and glorify the kingdom of God. See how God's word confirms this:

> *"There are different kinds of gifts, but the same Spirit distributes them. There are different kinds of service, but the same Lord. There are different kinds of working, but in all of them and in everyone it is the same God at work." (1 Corinthians 12:4-6)*

> *"All these are the work of one and the same Spirit, and he distributes them to each one, just as he determines." (1 Corinthians 12:11)*

> *"Now you are the body of Christ, and each one of you is a part of it." (1 Corinthians 12:27)*

> *"But you are a chosen people, a royal priesthood, a holy nation, God's special possession, that you may declare the praises of him who called you out of darkness into his wonderful light. Once you were not a people, but now you are the people of God; once you had not received mercy, but now you have received mercy." (1 Peter 2:9-10)*

CLOSING THOUGHTS

I trust God; I love Him and thank Him that He is able to use us as a light in so many areas of our life. We need to be witnesses for God in the world, not just in our church pews on Sunday, when we're all together talking about how much we love God. More importantly is the rest of the week as we go about our business… starting in our homes, starting with our wives and children, and going on to everyone we meet and everyone we encounter on the way. We are to be a witness and light for God, to glorify and reflect Him in all we do. If I can't say I am doing that, I believe I am failing in my mission as a Christian and failing in my mission as a child of God to do God's will here on Earth. So, it doesn't matter where God puts you; it doesn't matter if you're a night watchman, a star athlete, a teacher, a dog walker; it doesn't matter; job titles don't matter… hearts matter and minds matter. And hearts and minds sold out to God are truly the most beautiful things anyone can see. They are the most beautiful things God can see, and they will bring you all the joy, peace and pleasure that you desire in your life.

We pray this holiday season that is the desire of your life, and that is the kind of life you live. If it is, we salute you and applaud you and are proud to watch you in that life and be inspired by it. If you're not at that point yet, we pray that you take this holiday season to start spending some quiet time with God. Get with God one on one and just start reading and studying God's word, start praying and let Him reveal Himself to you. God says if we humble ourselves before Him, He lifts us up. Let's look and see what God's word says:

> *"Humble yourselves before the Lord, and he will lift you up." (James 4:10)*

> *"Which of you, if your son asks for bread, will give him a stone? Or if he asks for a fish, will give him a snake? If you, then, though you are evil, know how to give good gifts to your children, how much more will your Father in heaven give good gifts to those who ask him!" (Matthew 7:9-11)*

> *"Come to me, all you who are weary and burdened, and I will give you rest. Take my yoke upon you and learn from me, for I am gentle and humble in heart, and you will find rest for your souls. For my yoke is easy and my burden is light." (Matthew 11:28-30)*

Today, I look back (as I said at the beginning of this letter) to my friends who have passed away… Some of them I look back so sadly because it just seems like they were never happy in their lives, they never accomplished what they wanted to accomplish, they were always searching for something to make them happy and finally it was too late. Not only did they miss out on the joy of life when they lived it, but they missed out on the joy of an eternal life in heaven with God, simply because they continued to look everywhere else for their answers but to God.

So, I pray this holiday season that you don't make that mistake, that your life will be one that matters and counts and that you would let God bless you "abundantly and exceeding more than you could ask or imagine." It just starts with a simple hug from God, a simple encounter with the God of Creation, Himself. God is there. God created you. God wants to have that relationship with you. God is just waiting for you to turn to Him, waiting for you to come to Him and say, "Will you help me, Daddy? I love you, Daddy. Daddy, I'm broken. Daddy, I'm lost. Daddy, I'm scared. Daddy, I'm frightened. Daddy, I can't do it on my own. Daddy, I'm tired. Daddy, I can't make it. Daddy, I'm frustrated. Daddy, I'm angry. Daddy, I'm sad." I can promise you that God will respond, "Son, (or daughter) I love you. Come, let me restore you." God will indeed restore you to a life better then you could have ever imagined, both now here on Earth and then forever with Him in heaven. Look at God's own words on this subject:

> *"Seek the Lord while he may be found; call on him while he is near. Let the wicked forsake their ways and the unrighteous their thoughts. Let them turn to the Lord, and he will have mercy on them, and to our God, for he will freely pardon." (Isaiah 55:6-7)*

Our prayer is that you walk with the Lord and receive all the wonderful blessings from God this holiday season and every day. We should focus on how much we love God, not just at Christmas time, but each and every day of the year. I think the greatest joy and greatest peace I have in my heart is to know that I love God every day. I don't need a special day to celebrate and worship. I know God loves me each and every day of my life. Life is a joyful occasion, a joyful celebration; life has so much to offer. I'm standing on God's promise (and so should you) that not only is He with me every step of the way, not only has He planned my life out perfectly and has a purpose for it, but also that He has prepared a place for me in heaven when my life on Earth is over and I have nothing, absolutely nothing to worry about. It's just like the hernia surgery. It's all for good. See what God's word says:

> *"And we know that all things work together for good for those who love God." (Romans 8:28)*

This holiday season, it's in Jesus' name we pray for you and your family, and for all God's blessings to be upon you.

Love,

Jack, Beth, Ricky, Jackson, Talia, Skasha (the dog) & Noodie (the cat)

YEARGONE – a look back at…

2010

We are called to be His ambassadors even in the most difficult of circumstances on this earth. You see, God has called us out as His chosen ones to show the world we completely trust Him for victory even when we experience physical pain such as the debilitating pain I experienced with my hernia. How are you doing representing God through expressing His unfailing love to your family, friends and co-workers? As believers in Jesus Christ we must constantly remember that earth is not our permanent residence; we are simply passing through on this journey. Ask Him to help you love others today even in the most difficult moments of life. God hears you when you ask and will empower you with His strength to love others with the love of God.

2011

YOU COULD SAVE A LIFE

December, 2011

Dear Wonderful Family and Friends,

Happy Holidays, everyone! It is our joy to be writing to our family and friends this holiday season wishing you all a Merry Christmas, Happy Hanukkah and an awesome, joy-filled, Happy New Year to come.

Another great year has gone by and we, of course, will take a few pages to fill you in on the year past, life lived to date, and offer a glimpse into the future. All in all, you should find it mind boggling, mind bending, total lunacy or pure genius. Depending, of course, on your holiday mood and current view of the holiday season and the world. (Smile!)

ECONOMY

This economy I believe is the worst I've seen as an adult and worst I can remember. Those good people who tried to do the right thing and pay their debts have finally run out of IRAs, 401Ks, savings, home equity and credit lines. Many of our dear friends find themselves in dire financial conditions. We are praying for an economic miracle for them and our country… but clearly poor economic conditions have created "a new normal" regarding the standard of living. No longer can you be assured of short-term growth and profit from real estate or equities, and certainly there is no money to be made today by keeping our money in the bank. What's a fellow to do? Hang on to your money if you can, even at no interest. Better to have your cash with no interest, than to go for a big gamble out of desperation and lose! Our country is great. It will rebound. The south will rise again. It's just going to take time. So, the key for now is survival!

PAY ATTENTION…YOU MAY SAVE A LIFE!

On a more solemn note, a friend of mine in the solar industry committed suicide earlier this year. He was a fine and gentle man. I believe it had something to do with health issues, cultural issues and honor. But nonetheless, he chose to die. That broke my heart, as I believed he had so much to live for. It just goes to show you don't know what is going on in someone else's mind. With economic conditions so bad and many people hurting so badly both inside and out, it is our prayer that more people will turn to God for their peace, fulfillment, contentment, joy and place in heaven. But it is still our responsibility to be on the lookout and to reach out to any friends or family who may need someone to talk to or just need to unload about issues building up in their lives. I know you can't do it for everybody, but, if you can just help one person, I believe it is the best Christmas present you can ever give anyone. Just be there to offer a word of comfort, a bit of guidance, and perhaps direction to professional help if it is needed. Don't be scared to ask if everything is okay or not. You could save a life.

OUR MIGHTY GOD

I was visiting the mother of a friend and we were praying for her healing. She is true woman of God and has great faith. She told me she loves God so much in spite of her physical pain. How awesome is that!

That's where I want to be in my life… and where we should all want to be in life. She is so focused on Jesus and nothing else; all she sees is Him. There is other stuff to see in the world, but she focuses only on Jesus. No wonder she is so joyful, full of peace, loving and content, despite her pain. As she focuses on Jesus, she reflects the love of Jesus to others while fully wrapped in it herself.

Another friend is having a major issue with his eighteen-year-old son. His son wants to ignore his issues (drug use, lack of motivation, disobedience to his parents) and pretend they don't exist, or hope they go away. In my experience, guys who do that (ignore problems hoping they disappear) usually get crushed! I know my friend is heartbroken by his son's behavior, but he's more heartbroken by his son cutting off communication with him because the son no longer wishes to hear about his behavior, no longer wishes to be corrected and encouraged by his father to be shown a proper path.

He instead wishes to be left to his own vices. He is too stubborn and self-willed to know the outcome and see it as clearly his father does. I believe God, too, is heartbroken with us, like my friend for his son, when we shut him out of our lives. When we do that, it's like we are blocking the flow of God's love and blessings to our lives. The love and blessings of God are there for everyone, but when we turn from God, it's like a physical heart blockage where valves are clogged and stents need to be inserted or bypass surgery needs to be performed to open up valves. We need spiritual surgery on our hearts and God wants to operate on you today. Open up those clogged spiritual arteries and restore the full flow of God's love and blessings to your life. How do you do that? Simply ask it of God, turning back to him with a godly sorrow for your sin and for grieving God's Holy Spirit. Then you, like the prodigal son in the book of Luke, will be restored to the fullest of the graces if the Father immediately. Now that's my idea of a Christmas present for every struggling believer!

The Apostle Paul referring to the Old Testament said a veil of spiritual darkness (a spiritual blindness) prevented people from seeing the truth of God. That veil still exists today, as some are blinded to the truth of Jesus. But, God shows us the remedy to that today:

> *"Even to this day when Moses is read, a veil covers their hearts. But whenever anyone turns to the Lord, the veil is taken away." (2 Corinthians 3:15-18)*

THANK YOU, JESUS! That when we turn to you we can see clearly! The verse goes on to say… *"And we all, who with unveiled faces contemplate the Lord's glory, are being transformed into his image with ever-increasing glory, which comes from the Lord, who is the Spirit."*

Thank you, God, that your power transforms us with an ever-increasing glory that comes from you. What a great deal! The glory God gives continues to increase forever! Thank you again, Jesus! Listen, I have personally seen and tasted the Lord's goodness, received the benefit of his promises, guidance, wisdom, love, peace, joy, mercy and grace for twenty years now. It's the real thing, baby! God is alive. He is real. Try it; taste it for yourself. You will not be disappointed.

A few months ago, at a fiftieth birthday party for a friend, I had a little scare… a life scare. I had what seemed to be heart attack symptoms. I had them for a few days but I was sure it was not a heart attack. But a little less sure that night. (Smile!) So, although I thought I would be okay, I told Beth what was going on, in case my self-proclaimed medical diagnosis was wrong and I died. Fortunately, I was fine. (I must have pulled something.) Then I asked myself what would have happened if I had died that night and it reminded me to not take for granted one day or one minute of my life. I am to live it with joy and gratitude for the gift of life I have been given. I am alive now and will be for all eternity! Jesus alone offers eternal salvation and a new life. That little life scare with the heart symptoms that night reminded me we all have a terminal disease; it's called aging! But we don't have to die from it. We can live on forever with God!

So how am I going to live this life? Worried or happy? Sad, bitter or grateful? Mad or joyful? Concerned or amazed? For me it's a no brainer. I live all of it joyfully flopping around like a little kid in a foam pit. I am flopping around in the joy of the Lord, embraced by his grace, smothered in his love, covered by his mercy, forgiven of my sins and certain of my place with God in heaven forever (when my life on Earth is over and my work for the kingdom of God is finished on Earth). Now that is my definition of joy and happiness, unlike anything I've received from the world's definition of joy and happiness, (money, sex, alcohol, drugs, power, prestige, etc.) which ironically never made me joyful or happy.

ENCOURAGEMENT FOR GOD'S CHILDREN!

So, here's some great encouragement for every believer. My friend is a talented musician and wonderful man of God. But recently, he has been very depressed, feeling that he was letting God down by not using his musical talents to glorify God as much as he should. He wanted more opportunities to play and sing for God, but they just weren't coming. Satan used that as a way to get my friend discouraged. He felt like his worth as child of God was diminished because he did not use the skill set he believed was a gift from God. My friend told me the answer God gave him recently when he was in prayer regarding this very issue. He said God gave him a great and wonderful revelation.

God wants to do the same for you today. Here's what God revealed to my friend. God told my friend that he loved him because he is God's son, not because he uses his talents and gifts. God loves him because he's His son… even if he doesn't use his gifts and talents. Now, of course God would like us to use our talents for Him. That's why He gave them to us. But he doesn't love us any less when we don't. God loves us simply because we are His children. He sacrificed and died for us while we were still sinners because He loved us so much.

So this holiday season, remember God feels the same way about you. Don't let the devil trick you into feeling bad about yourself or separating yourself from the love of God… It's not about your accomplishments but your obedience to God. We simply must believe in Him. Out of that will flow your love and gratitude for all he has done for you, and out of that will flow actions that will glorify God and demonstrate to the world your faith in Him. That's what it's all about, my friends. God says we know a tree by its fruit. May your life and my life reflect the fruit and goodness of the Lord, so that all who see it and taste of it may be filled with the Spirit of God and taste and see His goodness and mercy!

I believe there is a true Christian revival that will take place. But, we must remember, revival starts with prayer! With godly men and woman coming to the altar and confessing their sins and repenting, coming to God with broken hearts, crying loud tears of sorrow, brokenhearted by our sinful condition. Then, leaving the altar of God changed, forgiven, encouraged and strengthened by the Lord.

As we see our righteousness as but nothing but filthy rags compared to Christ, we weep and repent because of the realization of how far short we fall compared to Christ and how grateful we are for His righteousness, His strength and His mercy. Then, restored to fullness with God, having fully repented and accepted God's forgiveness, we walk out, clothed in the righteousness of Christ — Holy, blameless and above reproach in God's eyes. Fully justified, we are repositioned closer to God's heart than ever before, never wanting to stray from Him again.

That's when revival begins in our lives as we focus our eyes, hearts and minds on the things of the Lord. As we seek His knowledge, it becomes our joy. As we eat of His words, they become our food and our hearts start raging like a fire for God. That fire for God starts to spread in our hearts and consumes us with His goodness and mercy and grace. Then, we too begin to imitate and reflect Jesus here on Earth. Then and only then can a revival begin in us and spread to others.

My Christmas wish for you is that God begins a personal and individual revival in your heart and that very spark catches on to become a wildfire in your heart, your house, your family, your city, your workplace and rages on for the rest of your life igniting all you encounter and meet. That's all it takes. I pray God starts with me, then knocks each of us to our knees like dominoes!

God says in 1 John 1:9, *"If we confess our sins, he is faithful and just and will forgive us our sins and purify us from all unrighteousness."*

I know on my own I am not capable of being the man God wants me to be or living the life God wants me to live. I have come to realize that I am tired of making promises to God I can't keep. I am tired of creating new plans and schedules for God I can't keep of my own power and will. I have come to the point finally where my prayer, and I hope yours today, is "Lord change me from within."

I cannot change my sinful flesh with my own power, but I can do it easily if I let God's power work in me. God was, is and has always been willing to change me for the better and make me into a more godly man. In the past, I was not willing to be changed in certain areas. After realizing I cannot bring about these changes on my own, I now know I can do it with the power of God. Perhaps your prayer mirrors my prayer. As we pray about our own areas of weakness in the flesh, say with all our heart… "Lord, I submit myself to you. I cannot change on my own. Please change my heart from within, Lord. Make it like yours. May I see the world and people, my family, my friends, strangers and all whom I come in contact with through your eyes, Lord. May I see them as lost children and love them as you do. Oh Lord, that I may decrease and you may increase, that I would die to myself and truly experience the full love and filling of Your Spirit in my heart, that I may live to imitate you, Lord. Oh God, please, please change me from within. Make me into the man you designed me to be." I can think of no other wish that brings more joy than being molded by the Potter into a person of impact and used by and for the Creator, who is our Lord and our Father and our King.

Recently, I took out a home equity line (on top of an existing mortgage) to continue to fund our solar project in North Florida and other ventures, so we had to see what our house was worth. Man did that hurt like heck. Not quite valued at what I had hoped. As well, the stock market has not been treating us well this year (although I felt a little better when I read that Wall Street stock guru John Paulsen was down 33% this year.) Still, cash flow stinks and the pressures on, so I was bumming out about that and feeling a little sorry for myself.

That same day I was driving along listening to the radio. It was a request show and the caller called in and said, "Hi, this is Harry from Philadelphia. I am a plumber. I want to request a song for my son, Harry junior. He is six years old. The song I request is "Tougher than the Rest" by Bruce Springsteen. You see," he said, "Harry, Jr. has cancer and every day he is getting treatment for it. He takes radiation, bone marrow transplants, chemo, and other drugs, and yet he gets up every day smiles and does what he has to do." The father said how much he admired his son's courage and toughness. Well my heart broke as I thought of my younger kids, Jackson is nine and Talia seven, and I just couldn't imagine them being in that situation, going through that. I cried and prayed for six-year-old Harry, Jr. God used that to remind me of how petty my financial woes are compared to some people's life issues and how lucky I am to be blessed with some financial concerns to deal with and not health problems!

Man, we moan and complain about the little things when some of us (me included) don't know what real trouble is. God refocused me and reminded me to be grateful for all things and that He was in control. As He said to His people in the old testament "have I not provided for thee?" He is still saying to us today! I refuse to worry or get upset or depressed about the future, about things I cannot control. I intend to focus on and control the things I can, work hard, love God and leave the outcome to Him.

One of my friends passed away over ten years ago, and I recently got a high school graduation picture of his daughter. She is all grown up. What a beautiful girl she is and it broke my heart that my high school buddy did not have the privilege and joy of seeing his beautiful daughter (and her brother) grow up. We are so lucky to be alive to have that privilege of seeing our children grow up. Man, we take so much for granted. My prayer this holiday season is that we make sure to take nothing for granted, especially those we love, starting with God and moving right to our wives, children and friends. In that order! How lucky we are to be alive, to be living life. What a blessing and privilege.

We have no problems, in spite of what we might see as issues or problems in our lives. We are so lucky, and here's why! It's directly from God's word. God has been breaking my heart with this verse over and over again these last few months, and I want to share it with you today.

> *"Blessed are those whose transgressions are forgiven, whose sins are covered. Blessed is the one whose sin the Lord will never count against them." (Romans 4:7-8)*

That's us! Blessed! That's the whole gospel of Jesus. Our whole lives right there. Could God be any more clear? We have received so much! Such a great and wonderful treasure - a relationship with the Savior.

Well that's it. I told you I would keep it short. (Smile!) There you have it. God is with us and from Him and through Him comes our joy and gratitude for we have all been forgiven. May your heart, mind, and soul be filled to capacity this Christmas with all the joy, peace, love, mercy, grace and forgiveness of the Lord. And may you remember to share some this holiday season with others less fortunate. God says it is better to give then receive… as always you can trust Him to be right. Do what He says; the blessings and rewards are amazing!

Be blessed, be well and enjoy. See you and talk to you soon. Hope you enjoy this year's gifts. God uses them to speak directly to your heart as we believe and pray He will.

Love,

Jack & Beth, Ricky, Jackson & Talia

YEARGONE – a look back at…

2011

Do you struggle with depression? Have you noticed hurting and oppressed people along your path in life? None of us is immune to the pain and suffering in this fallen world. This is why we must be AVAILABLE to one another for comfort, encouragement and guidance. We must actively choose to be the hands and feet of Jesus to our family and the world. Always remember, God loves you for who you are not because of your gifts and talents (which He gave you!). Get in His word today; read aloud a Psalm and share it with a family member. Taste and see the Lord is GOOD. How will you live your life? I CHOOSE to live joyful and happy, and I hope you do too!

2012

FIGHT BACK, RESTORE BALANCE

December, 2012

To Our Treasured Family and Friends,

Merry Christmas and Happy Hanukkah! We wish all of you a festive and joyful holiday season, and for that matter, a festive and joyful life! Why not… It's our wish, so we'll give you as much as we can!

We pray that everyone is enjoying good health this holiday season. We try to focus on the many blessings we have here on Earth, particularly here in America. Of course if you are lucky enough to live in Florida, it's even better. I've been across this great country of ours and, despite our inability to count votes in Florida, it is still the greatest place I have ever lived. Twenty-seven years in paradise!

FRONT PAGE NEWS

HURRICANE SANDY: Our hearts and prayers go out to our friends up north affected by hurricane Sandy's devastation. Of course we have had our butts kicked sufficiently over the years by Andrew, Charlie, Wilma and Katrina, so we can certainly understand and sympathize. These life-changing calamities are a reminder of how quick we can lose our possessions and the things we thought would always be there for us. That's a hard reality to face. A great reality to face is we can never lose God, no matter what. God said, "I am with thee always, I will never leave you or forsake you." Now that's a promise that can provide you great encouragement and strength here on Earth and one you can take with you to Heaven when you go to live with God for all eternity.

SCHOOLCHILDREN MURDERS IN CONNECTICUT: On the Connecticut shooting tragedy, the only comfort I can take myself or offer to anyone regarding that tragedy is the certainty that every child who was senselessly killed in Connecticut was in heaven that night having dinner with Jesus, and they will live with Him happily there for all eternity. We know God protects little children and covers them, and every young child is automatically granted a place in heaven with Jesus when they die before they were old enough to understand Jesus' sacrifice for their sin and thus make a choice to accept or deny Jesus on their own.

I want to share with you a few words from an e-mail my buddy, who I am providing consulting services for on his business, sent me the day after the tragedy: "Thank you, Jack, I will let you know when I drop off the business plan. More important than my business plan is the tragedy in Connecticut. I wanted to let you know my thought in light of what has happened today in Connecticut. It is this is beyond comprehension. More than ever, people need to hear the word you spread as the world is screwed without people like you. You definitely have your hands full to restore the balance. Sincerely, Brian."

My response to Brian and why I am passing it on to you, is not to pat myself on the back but rather to remind you, that it is up to ALL OF US to spread the word to this screwed up world. We spread it by the way WE live, and the things WE do and the actions WE take and the words WE Speak…we spread it by showing the love of Christ to all we encounter and hope that we can lead one person into the Kingdom of Light instead of them languishing as a prisoner of Satan in the kingdom of darkness. This is how WE fight back, but WE ALL need to do it. Not just me and a bunch of pastors — every child of God needs to be a useful weapon in God's hand, a useful soldier, ambassador, representative, and child of God. Our weapon is not guns, swords, or fists… rather it is the love of God, the Gospel of God, the Spirit of God shining through us as we put forth and pronounce the truth of God! Let's make sure WE do our part. Let's not go down as victims… let's fight for Jesus and righteousness as we would for our country and our family…even more so should we for God and His eternal Kingdom. Thank God for His eternal kingdom and our place in it. Perhaps we can stop the next senseless act of destruction, stop the next killer, stop the next child molester by bringing Him to a relationship with God through our witness before Satan gets ahold of him and uses him for destruction. That's how we fight back! Let's start fighting! Let's just tell everyone about Jesus and leave the harvesting to God. But let's make sure we do our part.

GODLY INSPIRATION

I want to share this famous prayer with you right now. It was written by a nun in the 1800s. I pray you meditate on these words and keep them as a daily reminder of God and His love for you. I do! You may want to (hint: YOU SHOULD!) tear this prayer out of our letter and keep it somewhere by your night table, on your desk or in your Bible, so we made it easy by making type big.

> May today there be peace within.
> May you trust God that you are exactly where you are meant to be.
> May you not forget the infinite possibilities that are born of faith.
> May you use those gifts that you have received,
> And pass on the love that has been given to you.
> May you be content knowing you are a child of God.
> Let this presence settle into your bones,
> and allow your soul the Freedom to sing, dance, praise and love.
> It is there for each and every one of us.

GODLY THOUGHTS TO REFLECT ON

I know life can get tough at times. As we deal with life's ups and downs, perhaps we need to consider the perspective of a friend of mine who recently drilled things down to this bit of insight he shared with me. "I believe it is best not to render natural judgments upon our circumstances and experiences, that they be 'good' or 'bad,' but simply see them as that which has come our way, and which is *to be blessed* by us so that we can *reap full benefit* from them. Most of us have a tendency to judge experiences or circumstances as 'bad' and as something to avoid or get away from, or as 'good' and as something to be drawn to and relished in, when it ALL should be seen as *neutral*, seen simply as things that have ultimately come to us *from the hand of the Father,* divine tools intended to be used by Him for our spiritual perfecting. I see now how many people today have to repeat the same trials over and over and over again, or seem to be stuck in their circumstances not moving on. This is because *these folks have not yet learned how to bless their experiences and circumstances,* how to see them from an eternal perspective, grow from them, and move on."

I think the above comments from my friend definitely merit some thought and meditation. See how they apply to your own life and the way you live and see if you agree with his thoughts.

Another friend, a retired policeman who now works and lives here in South Florida, was sharing his testimony with me the other day. He told me he was divorced from his wife and had two adult children. He said that before he knew Jesus, he was unfaithful to his wife many times and was a constant drug user, abusing drugs regularly until it all came crashing down. She divorced him. He had no relationship with his kids. One day, he found himself lying on his living room floor of his apartment (she had taken all the furniture in the divorce) and crying out to God. He cried, "God, I can't live like this anymore!" He said at that moment he felt the Holy Spirit of God embrace him. He felt a peace come over him. At that moment, he felt the Holy Spirit ask him what he had. He responded in confusion, as he had lost everything. But the Holy Spirit made him realize that he had everything he truly needed — shelter, food and most importantly, the Holy Spirit within him. He felt a peace and comfort like he had never experienced in his life.

The apartment carpet was old and smelly yet, at that moment, he felt enveloped by the Holy Spirit and filled with the unending mercy, forgiveness, peace, grace, love and joy of Jesus Christ. He said that carpet under His head felt soft and luxurious, as comforting as if it were a million-dollar rug. He said God made him realize he needed to focus on what he had, not on what he didn't have. He had God with him. That was five years ago and he has been an on-fire Christian since that very day. He is a changed man… transformed. His ex-wife told him she had been praying he would come to know the Lord. Her prayers were answered; he is a new man! What a great testimony and reminder to focus on how grateful we should be. All of us! Even those poor in money are rich… Even those poor in heart are rich. Only those poor in spirit with regard to the Lord are poor and broken!

These verses from Psalm 103 reminds us of God's everlasting greatness and mercy. Perhaps God will speak to you through these verses.

> *Bless the Lord, O my soul,*
> *And forget not all His benefits:*
> *Who forgives all your iniquities,*
> *Who heals all your diseases,*
> *Who redeems your life from destruction,*
> *Who crowns you with lovingkindness and tender mercies,*
> *Who satisfies your mouth with good things,*
> *So that your youth is renewed like the eagle's.*

For as the heavens are high above the Earth,
So great is His mercy toward those who fear Him;
As far as the east is from the west,
So far has He removed our transgressions from us.
As a father pities his children,
So the Lord pities those who fear Him.
For He knows our frame;
He remembers that we are dust.

As for man, his days are like grass;
As a flower of the field, so he flourishes.
For the wind passes over it, and it is gone,
And its place remembers it no more.
But the mercy of the Lord is from everlasting to everlasting
On those who fear Him. (Psalm 103:2-5,11-17)

GOD SPEAKING TO MY HEART!

I was at a concert recently… A Christian singer was talking about how great it would be to get heaven, see Moses and ask him how cool it was to have God's power to part the Red Sea. But then he said, "Before I could finish asking Moses about the Red Sea, he would interrupt me… 'Wait! That's not important! YOU tell me how it felt to have the Holy Spirit of God living in you twenty-four hours a day!'" Now that's a miracle! Remember in Moses' time, the Holy Spirit would fall upon people from time to time and empower or inspire them accordingly… But because the time of Moses was before the time of Christ, The Holy Spirit did not yet come to live inside of people. How can we complain when we have the Holy Spirit living inside us, empowering us and inspiring 24/7. That's crazy! Ridiculous! We should be the most on-fire, excited, happy, joyful people in the world. God is with us. LITERALLY! Oh, that you and I would just shut up and just enjoy the blessings we have been given. AMEN! When we have God, we already have everything we need. First Corinthians 4:8 "Already you have all you want! Already you have become rich!"

I have never in my life been so excited about the future, about seeing what God will do next and where He will lead us. I hope you feel the same about your life. I love the fact that change is coming and that God is in control! Hebrews 4:9 talks about resting in God. My pastor of twenty-two years and spiritual Father, Truman Herring, preached on this recently. If you are a Christian and not in a place of rest with God, you are missing out on the blessing God intended for all of His children! This place of rest exists. It is for Christians. He wants you to rest in Him, in His peace and His love and His finished work. *Hebrews 4:9-10* "There remains therefore a rest for the people of God. For he who has entered His rest has himself also ceased from his works as God *did* from His." Today and every day, for every child of God, God created a place of rest for us, for our hearts, minds, souls, bodies and spirit. Oh, that we would just shut up, stop thinking and start listening to God. How much easier and happier our lives would be.

Today I am meditating on Philippians 1:6, "He who started a good work in you will be faithful to compete it." God knew me before I was formed in my mother's womb. He made me. He formed me. It is by His will and His mercy and His grace that I live… He is faithful. He is righteous. And He does not lie. He will finish His perfect work in me. I have nothing to fear, and when I die, I will be made perfect in heaven like Him and be with Him forever and ever. So am I worried? No. It's time to rejoice! MERRY CHRISTMAS!

I want my life to be a reflection to others of the love I've received from Jesus. So that when people see me, or talk to me, or interact with me, they see and receive the love I have received from Jesus and it is transferred to them.

This year I read through the Bible in a year. It was George Guthrie's *Reading God's Story: A Chronological Bible*. (You can get the hardcover on Amazon, brand new, for about fourteen bucks) A good friend of mine gave it to me and it was such an amazing blessing. I have never felt closer to God as I read the Bible from a historical timeline perspective. I recommend you get it as a Christmas present for yourself and read it through this upcoming year. It was one of the greatest blessings I have received in my life. Day by day God opened my eyes to His truth and scripture. Even though I have read it all before, something about the chronological timeline aspect allowed me to perceive, receive and understand even more of God's word than ever. Plus, it got me spending time with God every day. I can't tell you how excited I was to be with God every morning. The clarity I received from going through the Bible from cover to cover was very fruitful. Give yourself the gift of God this Christmas.

THOUGHTS OF A DYING MAN!

AARP (American Association of Retired People) did a study... Here are the five things (in order of importance) people said they most regretted when they knew they were dying:

> I wish I had the courage to live a life true to myself, not the life others expected of me!
> I wish I didn't work so hard.
> I wish I had the courage to express my feelings.
> I wish I had stayed in touch with my friends.
> I wish I had let myself be happier.

Makes you think...huh? It should! Think about it now, not when it's too late!

MORTALITY AND CLOSING THOUGHTS!

An older couple I know well who are in their eighties were telling us at lunch one day how all their friends from their youth had passed away, and they were the only ones left. It seemed sad to me in one way — that everyone was gone and great in another — that they were still here. But you could see they were also considering their own mortality and realizing soon they too would join their friends, their time on Earth up.

They are such sweet and wonderful people and have treated me so specially all of my life; I love them so much. Yet it amazes me how different the attitude about dying is among Christians. As a Christian I don't fear death. I believe Jesus. I look forward to meeting Jesus face to face. I believe I will be with Him in heaven for all eternity. I have no fear. Of course I'd like to hang around and spend more time with Beth and the kids. (As you can see, it's fun!) but I have no fear of dying. On the other hand, many who don't know Jesus seem to me to be genuinely scared, uncertain, confused, anxious and worried about what happens after they die. And well they should… for they have no answer… no certainty… no assurance. That's sad to me, especially when I see it face to face with people I love. Nonetheless, all of us get to make our own choices in life. And that's the way it should be. I am just so grateful I know the way to the Father. I know the way to heaven and it is through Jesus Christ. I am in. My ticket was paid for by Jesus' blood on the cross, and that is why I am so happy and grateful to God and so joyful for whatever time I have here on Earth. Thank you, God. To God Be The Glory!

Five of my friends have died in the last ten years. The only thing that matters now is where they are spending eternity. Make sure you know where you will! For those of you who disagree, I understand and you have that prerogative. But if I truly believe what I believe, what kind of friend would I be to *not* share this with you?

They say it takes two to tango but only one to let go! God is holding on to you and He wants to dance. Make sure you don't let go! It stinks to dance alone! On that note I think I may take up flamenco dancing. I know it sounds crazy, but I can't get this image out of my head… black hat, black clothes (love it already) and dancing like a lunatic to Spanish music. We'll see if the urge continues. If it does 2013 may be crazier than even I imagined… But don't tell Beth. I want to surprise her!

Enjoy the CDs I've enclosed… Hope they motivate and inspire you to a closer walk with God!

GOD BLESS YOU ALL!

Love,

Jack & Beth, Ricky, Jackson & Talia

YEARGONE – a look back at…

2012

I am sure you agree that life can and does get tough at times. You cannot control everything (or most things!) that happens in your life. The question becomes: What are you going to do about it? How will you respond to the calamities in life? Take a moment to think about this, and write down your answer. I encourage you to see your life experiences from an eternal perspective…What can I learn here? How can I grow? How can I mature? How might God turn this situation around for my good? Focus on what you do have, and stop complaining about what you don't have. Start thanking God for His many blessings in your life, simple yet important ones like the air you breathe, electricity, your arms and legs etc. LIVE on-fire, excited and joyful because you realize God lives in YOU as a believer in Jesus Christ! One day you will see Jesus face to face!

2013

LESSONS I'VE LEARNED

December, 2013

Dear Wonderful Friends and Family,

I cannot believe this year has gone by so fast, but I am excited to write to you this holiday season. At our home, we continue to celebrate the wonderful gift of life we've been given by God and the happiness we enjoy with each other, reminding ourselves how blessed we are to be alive and to know God.

We really had a great year this year. In March I got to play professional Jai Alai. What a thrill! For six months, my buddy Wayne and I went to Miami every week to train and practice. In March, we went up to Hamilton County, Florida, and got to play professionally for one day. It was a great thrill and now I can cross it off my bucket list. *Hoof Beats* Magazine ran an article about it in their May 2013 issue so my place in history is secure (smile)! I have a world's record… I am the only man who has ever competed as a participant in two professional pari-mutuel sports. I've driven harness horses and now have played professional Jai Alai.

By the way, if Beth and I haven't told you personally, we love each of you and are praying for you. We know that many of you we don't see on a day-to-day basis, and sometimes just get to communicate on certain occasions. With some of our friends it's only with this letter. But just know that we miss you, we are happy for you and thankful that you care enough to catch up with us and take time to read about what's going on in our lives. Most importantly we pray that we are reflecting the glory of God and Jesus Christ in our lives and that you can see that our happiness, our joy, our peace, our contentment, our love, our life, comes from and flows out of our relationship with God. We hope you see our gratitude to Him for the gift of life He has given us... both the abundant life we have here on Earth, and the eternal life we look forward to forever in heaven, when our days on Earth are up. Thank you for being part of our lives. We pray we are a blessing to you...

This year I am sharing with you some very important things God has shown and put on my heart to share with you. They are in the stories below.

Merry Christmas & Happy New Year. God Bless You!

Love,

Jack & Beth, Ricky, Jackson & Talia

LESSONS I'VE LEARNED!!!

A LESSON IN LOVE

I will never forget one day this summer when we were in New York... Uncle Mike was taking Jackson shopping. As they were getting ready to leave, I noticed that Jackson was sitting in the front seat of Uncle Mike's car, which is something we had not allowed him to do yet (because he was not tall enough to meet the legal requirements to sit in the front seat in Florida).

When I said, "Jackson, get in the back seat." He immediately responded with authority, "But Uncle Mike said it was okay!" Although it broke my heart and I knew it would upset Jackson, I told him he could not sit in the front seat, no matter what Uncle Mike or anyone else said. I told him he had to get into the back seat.

Immediately Jackson began to cry. Clearly he was ready for a "big boy" moment (to sit in the front seat with Uncle Mike) and I had just destroyed any possibility of that. As sad as I was for him, and as much as I desperately wanted to give him what he wanted, I made a decision to put his safety and his life ahead of any short-term suffering he may endure.

As a father and a parent, I knew I was doing the right thing. While Uncle Mike is a great driver and has an incredible safety record, it was not Uncle Mike I was concerned about, but other careless drivers. We all know it just takes one time... one time not watching when you cross the street, one time not using a child seat in the back seat with a baby, one time not buckling your seatbelt, one time texting while driving, one time drinking and driving, one time using bad judgment... that can result in a lifetime of suffering or a life cut short.

The reason I am sharing this story with you this holiday season is to remind you that God your Father loves you and promises He's doing everything for your good, so that your joy will be complete. Yes, even those times when it seems like you're not getting what you want (like Jackson), even those times when it seems like you're ready for something and yet God doesn't give it to you, or tells you to wait, or even worse in our minds, tells you No! We still MUST remember the true love of God, trust Him, and know how much He loves us and how much He desires to bless us. As I know I was acting in the best interest of my son because I love him, I also know God acts the same way in our lives. I think when you realize that, see and understand it, it's so much easier to enjoy and accept life for all the wonderful things it is. It allows you to thank God in all circumstances for your know His hand is upon you. Look at this great promise from God in Jeremiah, and today He uses it to remind us how much He loves us.

> "Before I formed you in the womb I knew you;
> Before you were born I sanctified you... For I am with you," says the Lord, "to deliver you." (Jeremiah 1:5, 8)

A LESSON IN LIFE

My friend, Kerry passed away at fifty-four years old this year. God has shown me perhaps two of the most important lessons of my life through Kerry. When I met Kerry about fifteen years ago, he had a major problem with drugs and wound up in jail. He had thrown away virtually every opportunity life had handed him and there were many, including a wonderful set of loving parents who blessed him physically, spiritually, and financially with every possible blessing. Yet he was unable to conquer his addiction to drugs. I first went to meet Kerry and talk to him as a favor to his father, a church friend of mine. I remember meeting Kerry in jail that first day… After talking with him for over an hour, I left thinking, "There goes the hardest, toughest man I have ever met. There is absolutely no hope for this guy. He is beyond hope and nothing can change him or get through to him."

I was so convinced his situation was hopeless. I was tempted to stop praying for him, thinking what is the sense? Why waste the prayer? He has no shot! Yet it was through Kerry that God taught me one of the greatest lessons I've ever learned… as I watched God work a miracle in Kerry's life and turn him around completely. Kerry was transformed completely by God as he came crawling back to the Father like the prodigal son. I watched as God gave him victory over his addiction. I watched as Kerry then started and developed a successful construction company. I watched as he met and married a beautiful, devoted Christian woman. And I watched as God blessed them with two beautiful babies.

The lesson God taught me was to never stop praying for anyone or anything and never give up hope for anyone. The words of God are true, *"With God all things are possible." (Matthew 19:26)* God showed me that He was in control and He could change people, even when I had given up hope. With God, there was always hope, always a way out, and the power of God was indeed supreme, wonderful, and mighty. He could work anything according to His will.

From that point forward I made certain no matter how hopeless someone seemed, no matter how far gone I thought someone was, I was never to give up praying for them. God reminded me He changes people's hearts, in His timing and not mine. He showed me again, in a great way, *"that his ways are higher than our ways and his thoughts higher than our thoughts." (Isaiah 55:8-9)* Thank you, God, for that experience with Kerry. It increased my faith by leaps and bounds.

As the years went by, Kerry enjoyed his life immensely. Unfortunately, many years later, he fell back into the grip of those old addictions. It cost him plenty. It cost him his business, it cost him his health, it cost him his marriage, and I'm sure it cost him his walk with God, for it was clear that the peace and joy of the Lord had been removed from him.

We met one morning for breakfast, maybe a year ago, when he realized he was sinking fast and wanted to talk. I reminded him that Satan sought to steal, kill and destroy, and wanted only to suck him back into the pit of addiction and separate him from the love and peace and joy of the Lord. I talked about his two beautiful children and how, even if he couldn't do it for himself, he needed to do it for them. I referred to his kids, as I often refer to my own as "the faces." I said, "Kerry your life is all about the faces now. If you can't get sober and break free from your addiction for yourself, at least do it for the faces." He nodded understandingly, longingly and sadly and just said, "the faces."

Sadly he was unwilling to do what it took to get clean and sober for his precious kids ("the faces"), his wife or himself. Unfortunately, many people struggling with addiction are not willing to do what it takes. The answer is there; God does not lie. His Word is true and it says,

> *"No temptation has overtaken you except what is common to mankind. And God is faithful; he will not let you be tempted beyond what you can bear. But when you are tempted, he will also provide a way out so that you can endure it." (1 Corinthians 10:13)*

God was good to his Word, but the problem was Kerry was not willing to take God's way out and, at that sad and tragic moment, he was choosing his addiction over God's love. I offered him many paths to recovery including thirty-day rehab, ninety-day rehab, Narcotics

Anonymous, therapy, counseling, Celebrate Recovery, etc. He refused to embrace or engage any of them. It saddened me greatly, but I was even more shocked to learn, only six months later, Kerry had cancer and had only a short time to live. This came as a surprise to everyone; the diagnosis came out of left field. Just a few weeks later, I learned that Kerry was in hospice, so I went to visit him. I had no idea what to expect or what his mindset would be. When I got to his hospice bed, he was sleeping. I woke him up. I told him that I loved him and that God loved him and I read Scripture to him. The Word of God began to touch his heart and tears welled in his eyes. He couldn't speak but would moan confirmation as the Word touched his heart with a specific verse.

The great news was he knew for certain that he was going to be with God in heaven. He told his father a few days earlier he believed God had cut his life short because he had been disobedient, and this cancer came upon him as a discipline from the Lord. He believed God was calling him home early, with his life purpose on Earth unfulfilled. He knew clearly God had a better plan for his life, but that his disobedience had interrupted God's plan.

That was really sad, but what wasn't sad — and the greatest part of all, my second lesson and probably the most amazing one Kerry's life had taught me — was Kerry knew with certainty, he was going home to be with Jesus Christ in heaven. He knew his actions on this Earth were no longer relevant; all that mattered was that he was going to spend eternity with his Father, God who loved him and was waiting to embrace him. Kerry was standing with certainty on the promises of God. They were no longer promises he one day hoped to see. NO! They were promises he was seeing. This reality showed in the joy on his face and the certainty in his voice, even as he knew he had blown his opportunity here on Earth. He knew he could've done much better with his life, but now he relished, reveled and was excited about the certainty of spending eternity with Jesus Christ. I don't think I've ever seen a greater demonstration of the love of Christ or the certainty of heaven and the wonderful riches of glory, grace, and mercy of our Lord Jesus Christ as I saw with Kerry in his hospice bed.

Seeing the mercy bestowed on Kerry and knowing for certain — he and I both knew — the minute his heart stopped beating here on Earth, he was going to be with Jesus in heaven for all eternity brought great joy and certainty to my heart. I have always believed everything Jesus said, and I know for certain there is a heaven, but never has it been more clear to me how joyful it is as we transition out of this life into the next, how secure and definite our place is in heaven.

God used Kerry to show me another glimpse of His wonderful mercy and love. Psalm 103:12 was never more evident to me than that day at Kerry's hospice bedside. It says, "As far as the east is from the west He has removed our sins far from us." By the world's standards, Kerry may have wasted a lot of his life and made many serious mistakes that cost him greatly. No one could deny that fact. But the one thing he did that could never be taken away from him, the greatest thing he did, was he put his faith in Jesus Christ. He knew his faith in Christ was real and his relationship with Christ was real, and I knew it, too. Thus, as God promised, Kerry went to glory to be with his Father in heaven forever and ever, the most wonderful reward and true blessing for every believer in God.

Here's another great promise and reminder from God for you today!

> And it shall come to pass
> That whoever calls upon the name of the Lord
> Shall be saved! (Joel 2:32)

THE MOMENT LESSON

Here are a couple other things I've come to realize this year and want to share with you in the hopes that God will speak to your heart, touch your life, and give you greater insight and understanding to His will, His wisdom and His love for you.

I ran into an old high school friend of mine and we got a chance to reminisce. In his day in high school, he was one of the best looking and most personable guys you would ever meet. He had it all. He was funny, sharp, outgoing. He was a friend to all different types of people, from athletes to partiers to bookworms, and you would easily pick him as most likely to succeed. It seemed he always dated the prettiest girls. In fact, you could have looked upon him with envy, wishing that you were in his position, because at that point he seemed to have it all.

Now almost forty years later, he had let himself go quite a bit from thin, trim and fit, to quite a large man, and his hair was gone. I really had to look deeply into his eyes to make sure that, indeed it was really him, that he was still the same person… But he was. As we talked about life and family, it made me sad to hear that even though he had a career that allowed him to support his family, his marriage had disintegrated tremendously. He told me for many, many years and continuing today, he and his wife had not slept in the same bed although they were under the same roof. His own words to me were, "I am a recluse; I live in my room, most days I never go out. I can do my job from my room on the computer, so I never see anybody. I just live in my room and watch TV."

I thought how sad, yet he seemed perfectly content with his current life. I'm sure deep down he wished it wasn't this way, both in his physical appearance and how his life was being lived, yet he accepted it and seemed quite content with it. This reminded me of a drug rehab counselor's quote, "There's comfort in familiar pain." He has three kids and has lived the last twenty years of his life for them, but this too is changing as the kids grow up, leave home and have lives of their own. My buddy is left with himself in this isolated world he's created, alone yet accepting of his fate, and making himself comfortable with it. To me, it was very sad, dreams unrealized, potential unreached, marriage failed, remorseful, sad, yet willing to block it all out with food, TV and isolation. He was calling that existence… I call it slow death.

Why do I bring this up at holiday time? Because I hope and pray that you refocus your mind and your life. Focus on the moments we do have, not with regret or despair about the moments we don't have, not looking back wishing we could change moments that have already occurred (which we can't). Those moments are gone, and my life now consists of the moments I'm living in now… and so does yours! I'm happy with the moments I'm living now and I wouldn't trade them for the world. We certainly should not be focusing on the moments of other people's lives, or the actions and decisions they made, which we have no control over. While we care about them and have concern for them, our focus should be on the actions and decisions of *our* lives, the decisions and choices *we* make that affect our moments today. So, I come to you with excitement and inspiration this year to remind you to be grateful for the moments that you have, for our life is made up of this moment and other moments you are soon to live!

Remember, a football game is not made up of one play or one down, a basketball game does not consist of one shot, nor a baseball game of one at bat, nor does a song consist of one line, or a movie one scene or a book one chapter. No, it is the weaving together of all the plays of the game, of all the lines of the song, of all the chapters of the book that, indeed, make it a complete story. Isn't that our life, a weaving together of the moments of our life that make it our story?

We are not to focus on one bad moment in our life, or worse yet to be defined by one bad moment or one mistake. We are not to give up because of one mistake or even one hundred of them. But as the apostle Paul said, *"We are to press on toward the goal,"* (Philippians 3:14) and let history itself and God himself judge the moments of our life. We are, however, to enjoy them to the best of our ability and make the most of the opportunity we have to live. So remember, it starts one moment at a time, one day at a time. I pray that today you choose to live your day with joy, love, and peace. And watch, if you invest in the things of the kingdom of God, they multiply and compound coming back to you in ways you have never imagined, including but not limited to: joy, peace, happiness, love, mercy and abundant blessings from God… even more then you can ask or imagine, as God promises!

If you have any respect for me, any love for me, any kind thoughts of me, if you think I possess any knowledge at all about anything important, I hope and pray you will trust me on this matter, which is a matter of great importance for everyone — the quality of your life and how you live it! Don't get caught up in the circumstances, scenes and events of the world. That doesn't mean you shouldn't pay attention to them, just don't get caught up in them, for they don't define your life. The actions of your heart, the attitudes of the heart and the thoughts of your mind, these define your life. They tell us who you truly are! God says that out of the mouth come the thoughts and attitudes of your heart. I pray that your heart and my heart will be hearts filled with joy, peace, love, mercy, grace, kindness and comfort, to ourselves and others, that we may be a blessing and that every moment in our life may be of value for all eternity.

SELF-REALIZATION LESSON

I find sometimes in my own life I am so far from perfect, so far from imitating the life of Christ the way I want to. I find I am off track when I get upset with somebody, don't tell him what he did wrong, and then arrest him in my own mind. I try him in the court of my mind, convict him, and then sentence him to life in prison in my mind. What an idiot I am! I want to be a much better person than that, but I've learned that perhaps I will never be.

I realize there is sin living inside of me, and as the apostle Paul said, *"I do not understand what I do. For what I want to do I do not do, but what I hate I do." (Romans 7:15-16)* Yet remember it's not a sin to have a bad thought, it's just a sin to act on it. My job is to give those thoughts to Jesus Christ. God says I'm to take every thought captive and to give it to Him. So when those thoughts come upon me, I'm not to process them in my mind. Instead, I am to take that thought captive and give it to Jesus. I am, also through the power of Jesus Christ, to forgive that person who *I believe* wronged me… I do this not on my own, but through the power of God by the power of the Holy Spirit living inside me.

"For I can do everything through Him who strengthens me!" (Philippians 4:13) Remember, life is made up of our moments and focusing on the negative is not a productive way to spend them. So, since we are friends, I am sharing this with you in the hope you will see some of the moments you are not living the way you ought to or want to. I pray you would desire to seek God's power to have victory in your life in these areas. *"Who the Son sets free, is free indeed"* (John 8:36).

GOD ASKS ME FOR MORE LESSON

Recently in my quiet time with God, God has burned in my heart the specific verse *Matthew 6:33*, which reads, *"Seek first the kingdom of God and his righteousness and all these other things will come."* I was a little surprised, as this verse has been a "life verse" for me since I was thirty-six years old. So, for almost twenty years now, this verse has been a rallying cry for my life and my heart, and I believe I've truly tried hard to live it.

So I asked God, "What's going on here? I know this verse well. I don't have to revisit this verse; it's been my life verse from you God. I live it all the time." God answered me, as His Spirit spoke directly to my heart (not audibly, of course, but in the Spirit). God told me, "Yes, but you need to focus on the second half of that verse. It's not enough just to seek My kingdom first. You need to seek My *righteousness, as* well." (Emphasis mine)

As the weeks went by, it seemed that every day when I picked up the Bible to read in my quiet time, God's word would pop out at me as if it was in 3-D, highlighted and glowing. Every day, wherever I was reading there would be verses related to the righteousness of God. Many, of course, I'd read multiple times, if not hundreds of times over the last two decades. But now, as God will do, because His Word is alive in the hearts of believers each and every day, He brought a clearer meaning and understanding to the specific Word I was reading as it applied to my life today.

In His word God tells us we are to pursue his righteousness. He reminds us if righteousness could be gained through the law, then Christ died for nothing. He reminds us His righteousness endures forever. He reminds us that treasures of wickedness profit nothing, but righteousness delivers from death. Jesus refers to God as the righteous father. And finally after two weeks with the subject of righteousness burning in my heart every day, and God hammering me with Matthew 6:33, reminding me not only must I seek His kingdom first but also His righteousness, I knew God wanted me to go deeper. God had more in store for me. Now, I was always saying to God, "Lord, I want more of you." We know God says knowledge of the Lord is the beginning of wisdom. The more knowledge I get of God, the more I love him. The more knowledge I get of God, the closer I get to Him. God just continues to give more and more of Himself and since God is love, peace, mercy, joy, and grace… The closer we get to God, the more of those things we get.

It is an awesome experience and I am so grateful for knowing God since I was thirty-three years old. It just keeps getting better and better. So there I am last week in 2nd Corinthians chapter 5, in verse 21 and God brings it all home for me, as God knits the message together in my heart and explains it to me so clearly. It says "God made him who had no sin to be sin for us, so that in Him we might become the righteousness of God."

That's it! That's the message that God was sharing with me. We are to become God's righteousness here on Earth! It's not enough that we seek His kingdom… of course that's a good thing and a requirement for all Christians, but the truth for a maturing believer, one who wants to glorify God and live a life that is pleasing to God was now clear. God was showing me in my own heart, that this is what I need to do. It's not hard. I just need to do it. God said, "Jack you need to become my righteousness."

It's not enough just to be righteous when you want to, when it's convenient, or when you think it's a good idea. That's not what Jesus did; Jesus was all about his father's business all the time. Jesus actually embodied the very being of God His father and His very righteousness and represented it here on Earth when He came down in human form from His godly throne to live a sacrificial life for us — the perfect lamb without blemish, who gave His life to atone for the sin of all men. The sacrificial son… *"For God so loved the world that he gave his only begotten son that whoever shall believe in him shall never perish but have eternal life." (John 3:16)*

So, that's the message for me this holiday season and I hope God is speaking to you through it as well. It's my desire and my goal to start to live a life where I can become as the righteousness of God and I'm praying that God changes my heart, my mind, and my soul so that my thinking is aligned with Him 100% of the time. I pray that my joy continues to come from serving Him and pleasing Him and being a living sacrifice as Jesus was because I know this is what God desires from us and I know this is what brings the greatest joy to God's heart and will give us the most wonderful blessing ever both here on Earth and forever in all eternity.

I know God is real. I know He's not a liar. I thank God that He is showing me this holiday season what the next step is for me in my life. I'm not saying the next step for you in your life is to become the righteousness of God (though clearly I believe that message is for every single believer in Jesus Christ and that's what we should all do). But I do know this — God wants us all to take the next step wherever we are. He wants us to advance in knowledge, in wisdom, in action, in truth, and in spirit. And we do that by going forward with whatever instruction the Holy Spirit is giving our hearts! In other words, don't just listen to God, do what He says! We do that by responding to the call of the Holy Spirit in our believing hearts.

I pray first of all you would be opening up your Bible and let God's words speak to you, in a quiet time when you shut out the distractions of the world so that you can hear the quiet whisper of God. And when God whispers to your heart about what He would have you do next in your life to come closer to Him, that your responses is always, "Yes, Lord, yes." I can tell you that's where the true blessing of joy and pleasure and the true meaning of living life comes from. Don't miss out on that. As I believe that's the greatest gift God can give you this holiday season.

REMEMBER THIS: You don't become faithful in order to be loved by God and be free…you are already free and loved by God and that's why it's possible to be faithful! Here's the last thought for the year and one I hope God will touch your heart with like He has mine.

> *I love those who love me,*
> *And those who seek me diligently will find me.*
> *Riches and honor are with me,*
> *Enduring riches and righteousness.*
> *My fruit is better than gold, yes, than fine gold,*
> *And my revenue than choice silver. (Proverbs 8:17-19)*

KEEP THE TRAIN ROLLING!!!

Love,

Jack

YEARGONE – a look back at…

2013

Sitting at my friend Kerry's bedside in hospice was a pivotal life moment for me. I learned a couple of important lessons from God such as never to give up on anyone and to keep praying and believing. You see, one word from God can change a situation in an instant. One word from God can transform a heart for all eternity. Thankfully, Kerry placed his faith, his full trust and confidence, in Jesus Christ for forgiveness and eternal life. He is with God in heaven. So, who is the 'Kerry' in your life? Who is God asking you to pray for and keep believing Him for a miracle? I encourage you: DO NOT GIVE UP. KEEP PRAYING. KEEP BELIEVING. God is faithful to His Word.

2014

THE BOTTOM LINE

December, 2014

Hello, wonderful family and friends.

It is great to be able to write you as we close out 2014 and celebrate another year of living. I pray that indeed you are celebrating living, that your life is a celebration, a joyous journey and one filled with excitement, hope, adventure and love. A few laughs wouldn't hurt either!

Well, instead of the usual sixteen-page missive on life, I have decided to boil things down this year and really focus on the bottom line. With time so valuable and in short supply, and life so full of clutter, distraction and responsibilities, it seems these days, getting to the bottom line is not only beneficial but a requirement. Nobody has time to waste. So, here's this year's bottom line.

LIFE... Imagine getting the opportunity to eat a beautiful meal, a wonderful awesome gourmet meal, and not allowing yourself to enjoy it because you wanted something else, or someone else criticized it or said it wasn't any good. I think that's our lives sometimes. We have this amazing life, but we always look at what we don't have instead of what we do have. We focus on what we don't have and make ourselves miserable. Or we let a comment or thought of someone else's definition of reality or what we should enjoy, or how we should enjoy it, affect and impact our own lives, causing us to miss the greatest blessing we have, which is indeed our lives. So, the bottom line is enjoy your life; it's the only one you get!

LOVE... People can choose to make each other happy or choose to make each other miserable. Why be miserable? Especially if it's a choice. I challenge you this year to choose to love and forgive, and choose not to criticize and blame. It seems reprehensible and ridiculous that we would make miserable those closest to us — our spouses and family. I say it again — to love is a choice. To be kind, gentle, forgiving, merciful, truthful, generous, gracious, live with integrity, these are all choices. Choose to love and I am certain you will be amazed at how much you are loved.

KIDS... Enjoy them while you can... Enjoy the many phases of their growth and development. Don't wish so quickly for this phase to pass and the next phase to begin. Because you will soon miss the phases that you had and wonder how they went away so quickly and where the time went. I've been blessed to have the privilege to be around my kids as they grow and develop and can't believe how big they are getting. Ricky is twenty-six and married, Jackson is twelve, and Talia is ten.

But I'll tell you one regret I won't have is that I missed spending time with them because I am spending time with them. I am far from a perfect father, and I'm told constantly by Jackson and Talia that I worry way too much. (I think I inherited that from my mother.) But one thing they will never be able to say is that I didn't love them enough. I am making the most of the time with my kids; what a joy it is.

It doesn't mean you don't discipline them, worry about them, correct them, train them, nurture them... of course you have to do all that stuff. But don't get so busy thinking about what you have to do that you don't spend that individual one-on-one quality time with them, getting to know who they really are. Also, remember when you were a kid? Your parents couldn't tell you what to think and when you got to a certain age they couldn't tell you what to do. Surely, our kids are no different. Enjoy them, love them, pour into them, teaching them everything you know and then pray really hard... because that's really all you can do.

PURPOSE... I believe this is a critical area of a life well lived. To have a purpose is a key to life. It seems to me that people commit suicide (like Robin Williams and others) when they have no hope tomorrow will ever be better than today. For me, as a believer in Jesus Christ, (and I believe for every believer in Jesus Christ), our lives and purpose are clear. We are to live a life that glorifies God. We have a purpose in our life and we feel that we are living a fulfilling life and our life has meaning. What a great blessing to be a Christian and have that certainty. If you don't have that, then having another purpose will still allow you to have a better life than not having a purpose. It may be a professional purpose, a personal purpose, but it is a primary reason for living and always brings you great joy, satisfaction and fulfillment when you are pursuing it.

PASSION... Another critical key to a happy life is passion. Without passion (I don't mean physical passion, I mean a passion for life) life is frustrating, disappointing and depressing. Imagine a singer passionate about singing who instead works as a cashier at a supermarket. Or a doctor passionate about providing the best healthcare to people, who parks cars for a living. Of course they can do those other jobs well. But they never escape from sadness and longing of what might have been and what should have been, as they realize they are missing out on what they were created to do. The haunting reality every day that you are not following your passion and inspiration for life can be a critical factor in sucking the life, joy and hope out of person. So live with passion or with purpose... I hope you have both. Otherwise life seems so meaningless and, unfortunately, with that perception, it truly can be. I hope you will seize this moment to make it your primary focus and intent to live the remaining time of your life with passion and purpose. For therein lies an important key to life and happiness.

WORK... I had dinner with a very wise and well-respected man the other night, and somehow the conversation came to businessmen, making money, and people profiting from things that were just cruddy, wrong or deceitful. He asked this question, "Couldn't people just take their talents and make money by doing something that is good and helps people?" And that's the question for us. Is what we are doing being done with a desire to truly help people? Aren't there enough ways in the world to make money helping people? We shouldn't have to do it hurting people or ripping them off.

ENJOYMENT... "Time is an ocean... but it ends at the shore!" So don't be an idiot... Enjoy yourself now!

DEATH... Years ago, Jimmy Breslin was a sports columnist for a New York newspaper. He was the most respected odds maker in the world of sports handicapping. Yet he once said, "I wouldn't wish on my worst enemy that he gambled" referencing the fact that he knew the pain, frustration and torture a gambling addiction would bring. Even though he was the man who set the odds, he knew all too well the turmoil, pain, anguish and torture of a gambler's life (it's the same for a drug addict or alcoholic).

With that same thought process in mind, I wouldn't wish on my worst enemy that he has not resolved the issue of what happens when you die. The death issue! To me it's a simple equation. If you don't believe in God, you might as well do whatever you want on this Earth, with no restriction, no conscience and no concern. For this is the only life you're going to get. If there is no afterlife (heaven), do whatever the heck you want and enjoy the short sixty, seventy or eighty years you get on Earth. However if you do believe, as I do, that there is a God (for me that is our Father God in heaven, who gave his son Jesus Christ to die for our sins on the cross, so that by believing in God's son Jesus we live eternally with God forever when our time on Earth is finished), then how awesome it is to know that when you die it's just the beginning of your life. I have that assurance in my heart, in my spirit, in my soul, in my mind and in every fiber of my being. I believe that is the greatest gift I have ever received… What a joy! Thank you, God. That said, I repeat, I would not wish on my worst enemy that he did not have and know the certainty of spending eternity with God in heaven.

SUFFERING/SICKNESS… Batteries go dead, new parts get old — some you can fix and some you must replace. Some you can't and the product (toaster, car, person, etc.) is dead and gone forever. Now useless, it must be thrown out. Our bodies are rentals, and at the end of the ride we turn them in. In the past I've had back surgery to fix my back, hernia surgery, which repaired my hernia and this year stem cell shots in my shoulder, which repaired my torn rotator cuff. Now, I feel amazing. However, there is no doubt that I too will suffer from more sickness or illness if I live long enough. As well, I am certainly going to die a physical death one day. This is a part of life. Like when we go through a painful root canal, we don't enjoy the process, but we certainly enjoy the benefit after the root canal is over. We enjoy not suffering anymore, not having pain in our teeth, and being able to chew freely and enjoy great food. So, we see temporary pain or suffering can produce a long-term benefit. So for us, much like a football player getting tackled, or an emergency room doctor getting blood on his hands, it's just part of the game of life. Isn't it great to be alive to go through these things? I think the answer to that question will determine whether you are joyful or miserable as you go through life. My answer is yes… It's great to be alive and playing in the game of life.

POLITICS… Liars, liars, liars. Perhaps their intentions were good going into politics, and they thought they could make a difference in the world, but I've yet to meet one who wasn't corrupted by it all. I guess it just makes them human. I wish everybody would be inspired and required to do their jobs as excellently and as honestly as possible, with no self-dealing, but our system's not perfect.

That being said, I have to accept the system as it is, whether I like it or not, because I certainly am not willing to dedicate my whole life to changing it. This is yet another price we pay to be alive. I would still rather be here in America than anywhere else. I still believe it's a great country. To God be the glory! We still have freedom, even though the government knows our every move now with the advent of technology. (Yes, your computer and phone are spying on you!) But, the bottom line is if you're not doing anything wrong, you really have nothing to worry about. Unless of course you just want to waste your time in life thinking how unfair and wrong it is. Personally, I'd rather spend my time in life being productive and loving and making a difference where and when I can.

PEOPLE... Well, I love people and I have come to learn that their love for me is conditional, based on my behavior. I understand that. I get it. If I do things people like, they like me. If I do things they don't like, then they don't like me. Unfortunately, I am exactly the same way when it comes to them. I thank God that His love for me is unconditional. It gives me a greater perspective on dealing with people, family, friends and strangers. I try to see them through God's eyes. I try to be like Jesus. Practicing love, forgiveness, mercy, grace, kindness and generosity to those I meet, and whose lives I touch. I didn't say I was good at it, but I'm trying! (Smile!) I don't think we can ever change that basic human nature in us that makes us love so conditionally, but I believe we can certainly change ourselves for the better and we can become the people we want to be. I think that's the goal. To live a life of impact, a life that matters, a life that counts at the very least to God, and hopefully to those around you and to the world.

FINAL THOUGHTS… Scott Satloff was an American journalist who was killed this year by ISIS terrorists. You may recall from newspaper headlines and videos that Satloff was the second American journalist beheaded by the terrorists. While in captivity Satloff managed to smuggle two letters home to his family. Here's a portion of what he wrote, "Everyone has two lives, the second one begins when you realize you only have one." From captivity he also offered this wisdom to loved ones, "Do what makes you happy. Be where you are happy… Love and respect each other. Don't fight over nonsense… Love and respect each other. Eat dinner together… Live your lives to the fullest. Stay positive and patient. God rewards those who are patient."

I share that with you as a final reminder of the bottom line. It was Satloff's message to his family, what he believed was most critical for them to know. Facing certain death, he wanted to send one last message home. Wanting to get across what was important, what mattered, in essence the bottom line. Please take his words to heart this holiday season pray on them, meditate on them and see if they would inspire you to refocus your own lives on what is truly important. I pray that we would not need some life-ending, life-threatening tragedy, illness or incident to cause us to grab hold of what's really important.

Remember Psalm 63:3 says, *"God's loving kindness is better than life."* If you believe that then you will never have any reason to get down, to give up, to be depressed, because you will you already have everything." In Isaiah 26:3 God's word promises, *"You will keep him in perfect peace, whose mind is focused on you."* Could God's instructions be any clearer? You want perfect peace, stay focused on God.

So, that's it for this year. I think I've given you the bottom line on everything. Everyone will usually tell you all that counts is the bottom line! That's the point this year. God bless you. Have a great holiday season and a happy healthy new year. Keep the train rolling!

Love,

Jack & Beth, Ricky, Jackson & Talia

YEARGONE – a look back at…

2014

So, how about you? What is your purpose for living? What is your passion that enables you to jump out of bed each morning in excitement? What were you created to do on this earth? Take some time to journal your thoughts. Then, seize the moment. Take action. You have ONE amazing life to live. Make it count for all eternity. Use your gifts and talents to help people as you have opportunity. Give it your all. Be productive, love and make a difference. Live a life that makes a difference. One that counts for all eternity and for all eternity you will be glad you did.

2015

LIFE ON THE MOVE

December, 2015

Hello to our dear family and friends,

Merry Christmas and Happy Holidays 2015! We hope and pray you are all getting excited about the coming year and are eager to see what God will do in your lives. We've had an amazingly strange and wonderful 2015 and are filled with joy, happiness, and delight as we reflect on what has transpired. Some of it is quite incredible, and some of it you may find rather astonishing. I can assure you of one thing — all of it actually happened.

BIG NEWS!

Beth and I became grandparents this year as our son Ricky and our wonderful daughter-in-law Kristi had their first child. We have never really experienced anything like this before. Perhaps by the time you read this we will have made our initial visit to see this precious, wonderful, new person who has captured our hearts before we even held her hand.

THE BIG MOVE!

Speaking of people on the move, God has spoken to our lives and hearts in a mighty way this year, which resulted in our relocation to the Orlando area in September. We now live in the beautiful town of Windermere, Florida. The bottom line is God has been pressing on my heart for over a year that we are supposed to come to this area and help a buddy of mine who is starting a church. After much prayer, God knitted Beth's heart together with mine on this, and we made the decision to move. The day after we decided to move, a buyer came and bought our house. That was after two and a half years of the house being on the market without one single offer, not even a low-ball offer to turn down. We clearly saw God's hand moving when we stepped out in faith and took off the restrictions and conditions. (Like Abraham offering up Isaac, like Noah being faithful to build the ark even when people thought he was crazy, and like the apostles who left everything to follow Jesus.) We in essence finally said to God, "We're in no matter what." The interesting (or insane) part was the buyer gave us just two and a half weeks to move out. So, by September 4, we had packed up and moved to Windermere.

Talia and Jackson are just amazing. They are writing restaurant and movie reviews as part of a family fun competition. Jackson is a walking encyclopedia when it comes to weapons and their history. Talia's artwork and drawing is amazing. Being with them is so much fun for Beth and me. It's as if our life is a living sitcom… and we love comedy!

Those of you who have been to our old house know it was a very big house. It was quite a task to pack thirteen years of living and move out of six thousand square feet. But we did it! It was unbelievably strenuous, stressful, and exciting at the same time. I can't describe to you the exhilarating feeling of being involved in something God is doing — that thrill of something new. I equate it to when I first went off to college. I knew I wanted to go. I knew it was the road to take, but I wasn't sure what lay ahead or how it would unfold. I experienced the same nervous excitement when I graduated college and came back to New York to start my career on Madison Avenue — the certainty that you're on the right road but you don't know what lies ahead. I had the same feeling when I moved down to Florida in 1985. But this year I clearly felt God saying to my heart, after thirty years of living in south Florida, it was time to finish that chapter of our lives and start a brand new one. We are so excited to see what God will do.

Of course it is never easy to leave friends and family behind, and we especially miss all the quality time we got to spend with my mom and dad every week. We still go down once a month to see them and stay for a weekend, but under no circumstance do we want to miss the blessing God has in store for us. We did not want to get into that "prevent defense" mentality of holding onto what we have. We know for certain any time a team plays a prevent defense, they invariably lose the lead because they stop doing the things that got them points on the board (being aggressive and playing offense) and start trying to protect what they have. So, no "prevent defense" for us… Damn the torpedoes! Full speed ahead!

ARE YOU KIDDING ME, LORD?

In May of this year, we found out that Beth was pregnant. We were shocked. She had an IUD and we believed that pregnancy was impossible. However it was possible! God's Word does not lie. He says, "All things are possible with God." After the shock wore off, we prayed. We knew we were unprepared to have another child (Jackson is thirteen, Talia is eleven, and Ricky is twenty-seven — married and a father) We could not imagine the thought of bringing up a baby and going back to that time in our lives. As we prayed, we felt a supernatural peace knowing that God is God, and if it was truly His will for us, we would love this child and make any sacrifice necessary because we trust the Lord. Even though it wasn't our plan, if it was God's plan, we were on board. We became excited about this amazing miracle of God. However, it was not to be as it was not a viable pregnancy. This will be the second child I get to see for the first time when I get to heaven as we had a previous miscarriage before Jackson was born. Why do I tell you this? Simply to show you that whether or not it is our plan, whatever God brings we want. It's Proverbs 14:12, "There is a way that seems right to a man, but in the end it leads to death."

I want to tell you how proud I am of my wife, her faith and devotion to God and to our family. She was willing to accept God's plan like Sarah and, even though she didn't understand it like Mary, if it was God's will she was all in. Her faithfulness in following God's call, leaving behind her friends and the life she built in south Florida over the last seventeen years, to go to Orlando, forsaking all to answer God's call, was a great inspiration to me and makes me love her even more…although I thought that was impossible. See, God was right. All things are possible with God! Seeing God knit our hearts together and feeling God's hand on our lives and our hearts brings us tremendous joy.

More of What God Is Doing…

TRUEST OF TRUTH!

A few weeks ago, I had the pleasure and privilege of seeing my wonderful cousin, Gary. I love Gary so much and I have only seen him two times in my life, last week being the second time. Gary was born with Down syndrome and lives in a residential home in upstate New York that provides for all of his comfort, needs, and care. He's in his fifties now.

A few years ago, we had a family Passover celebration at our house in Florida and had the joy of meeting Gary for the first time and spending a few days with him. He touched my heart in such a big way. His innocence and love for people and life was so pure and true and unpolluted. It brought great joy to my heart to talk with him, to laugh with him, to hug him, to share ice cream with him, and just to see how happy and satisfied he is simply being alive. No panic about the past, no concern for the future, merely living in the joy of the moment and responding to each second and event as it occurs. I couldn't help but think back to the Bible passage in Matthew 18:3 were Jesus says we are to accept the kingdom of heaven like little children, with the complete belief and faith of a child, taking to heart every word their father says. Gary does just that.

I have not forgotten my visit with Gary a few years ago, as it touched my heart deeply and impacted me tremendously. When I found out he was going to be in the Orlando area on a trip with his residence home, and that my aunt and uncle would be coming up to visit him as well, (as they do every year) I was delighted to be invited to have dinner and spend some time with them.

We met for dinner last week and I just want to share with you the hugs I received from Gary. The warm, genuine, loving hugs and the delight and happiness he expressed about seeing me. I believe it was the closest thing to the pure love of God I will ever see here on this Earth. I am so grateful for it. As Gary hugged me, we spoke more with the hugs than with words (although we spoke plenty with words and that was great, too). I could feel it in every inch of my body, every particle of my being. I felt as if I was hugging Jesus himself, as Gary's love overflowed and overcame me in the most wonderful way — a sweet reminder of the purity, fullness, and completeness of God's love.

I've lived a very full and active life. I partied way too much in college, followed by an advertising career on Madison Avenue. Since moving to Florida, I have had many successful business ventures, along with some not-so-successful ones. I preach and write books, but most importantly I hope in these last twenty-four years since God came into my life I have made it a priority to care, share, love other people, and help them any way I can. Others may look at me sometimes in envy and say, "Hey, Jack, you live this great, amazing life." Yes, it's true; I have. Many things I've done in my life have given me great pleasure (for example: racing harness horses, playing softball, being a Madison Avenue advertising executive, going to Yankee fantasy camp, Springsteen concerts, along with a host of other wonderful things). Even better and more important than those experiences are all the people I've had the joy of knowing, the relationships I've had, and the friends and family I've had the opportunity to walk through life with — some for a season and some for all my life. What a joyful, wonderful, happy life I have had, made more full and complete by my wife of fifteen years, Beth, my three wonderful children, Ricky, Jackson, and Talia, my new daughter-in-law and now my precious new granddaughter. God opened this new chapter of my life, and I am excited to see what He has planned for our time in Orlando. I don't know if we'll be here for a year or the rest of our lives, but I do know that we are walking with God and that is the only place I want to be. It is both thrilling and invigorating, but it also brings a peace and joy, a true treasure that cannot be bought. Yet of all those experiences in my life and all the wonderful things I've done, I rank the hugs I received from my cousin Gary as one of the best!

Isn't it amazing that until he and I both get to heaven, he may never realize the impact he had on my life. Others may look at him and think, what a shame he had to live this way. I say, "Oh no, what a blessing.

God created him with a purpose." I believe one of the purposes of his life was to show me the love of God through his life and I am so grateful to God for that. I pray that you and I would align our hearts with God and enjoy the simple joys and pleasures God has given us in our lives. We should live in an attitude of gratefulness and appreciation and excitement for what today brings, enjoying each moment and not burdened by the passing of time, not wearied by unmet expectations, and not murdered by fear of the future… Just alive, being, living, loving, laughing… So thank you, Gary, my brother and cousin, (God's child) for sharing your love so freely and for reminding me what really matters!

LIFE'S GREAT LESSON!

Here in Orlando I got to plug in with my buddy Sean who is a pastor and looking to start a church. (He is the friend God was pressing on my heart to help here in Orlando.) He invited me to join his weekly men's ministry group, which consists of about fifteen hard-core Christ-centered men. I met Tim, a fifty-year-old man who is dying of cancer. According to the doctors' diagnoses, he had less than four months to live. The first few times I saw him at these weekly group meetings, he didn't say much. But I could see the love of the other men for him, the care and concern for their brother, and I could see that it was his desire to live his life as normally as possible, attending these meetings in spite of his physical pain.

Then one week I had the pleasure of sitting with Tim (and my buddy Sean) for some coffee. We talked for a few hours and he shared with me a lot of his life story, about his love for God and his family, about facing this illness and continuing to pray for a miracle of healing from God, but preparing for the fact that God may choose to heal him in heaven, in which case he will be saying goodbye to people and things on Earth. He was most concerned for his wife, his kids, and grandkids.

I asked him what he would like to do in the time he had left, if there was anything specific, anything on his bucket list, hoping that perhaps he'd share something we could make a reality for him. His response astounded me and motivated me like nothing else I've ever heard in my life. I believe I could've studied my entire lifetime, with scholars and prophets, saints and pastors, and never heard articulated what he said to me in one simple sentence. So let me share it with you as a gift from Tim to you this holiday season.

Tim told me that when he first got the cancer diagnosis two years ago, he and his wife went into their retirement savings to take a three-week Alaskan cruise with their family and loved ones. He said it was an amazing time of fellowship, bonding, and closeness with his family, something he will always treasure — the great blessing of time with his family. He shared in that regard his sickness, the cancer, had truly worked to bring the family closer together as little things that used to get everybody so upset were pushed to the background. Quality time, love, and just being together were of prime importance as they realized the most valuable assets they had were God and each other.

A few months ago the doctors gave him a six-month to live prognosis and he knew it was all the time he had left. He had started to really begin to feel cruddy and could feel the physical symptoms taking their toll. Now he walks with a cane, has very little energy, and his body is slowly deteriorating. So when I asked him the question of what he would like to do he said, "What I would really like to do with whatever time I have left is to pour into people's lives with the love of God because that's the one thing I won't be able to do when I get to heaven." I thought, man what a great perspective, what a great reality... Isn't that the way we should all be, all the time with every moment of our lives? It shouldn't take a specific wake-up call from life for us to remember Psalm 39:4, "Show me Lord, my life's end and the number of my days; let me know how fleeting my life is." It shouldn't take a tragedy or staring death in the face for us to have that attitude. Oh Lord, let me know the days of my life that I may focus on you!

I was reminded, inspired and encouraged by Tim's faithfulness to God, his love for his family, and most importantly his desire to live a life that mattered for God by fulfilling God's purpose for him. It wasn't about him, but about loving others, just as Jesus did. He is a living example of Jesus Christ here on Earth.

I hope you will join me in praying that God performs a healing miracle in Tim's life and we can have an even greater testimony of God's power at work in his life. But I tell you I have already seen the power of God at work in his life and I know Tim has seen it too. He also said to me and Sean, "If my sickness can impact one person for the kingdom of God, if it can help bring one person through that narrow gate to a relationship with Jesus, to an abundant life here on Earth and in heaven with the Father forever and ever, if it can bring one person closer to Jesus then it will have been worth it. And I would gladly do it again." I do not believe I have seen such faith anywhere on this Earth.

If the whole purpose for God bringing me to Orlando was to learn that lesson from Tim, about what is important and how to live life, then it is more than worth it already. And Tim, you are spending your remaining time pouring into people with God's love and I am so blessed to be one of them. Thanks, buddy!

CLOSING THOUGHTS

In the ten weeks or so we have been in Orlando, God's hand has appeared to me in so many places. God has spoken to me through so many wonderful people here, and I clearly see the power of God alive and at work. That is not to say the same thing doesn't happen in south Florida and all around the world; of course it does. God is alive in the heart of every believer, and He created the world so that all would be in fellowship with Him. But I believe God has given me a heightened sense of awareness, a heightened sense of His presence, and it has nothing to do with Him being any more present than He ever was. As we know, God is the same yesterday, today, and forever. This has to do with my heart, and my eyes and ears being aligned more closely with God. All of God's Word is true and we should take James 4:8 to heart this holiday season. "Come close to God, and God will come close to you." That's a promise from God to you. What an incredible gift!

I've enclosed a few CDs for you this year. One of them is titled *Orlando* and talks about our move and how God moved in our lives. God has impressed on me through many individual instances, people, and circumstances throughout the past ten weeks, not only of His presence, but of something He wants to teach me so that I would have the benefit of it and receive even more of His blessings, and that's this…God wants me dependent on Him at all times, not just the critical, important times when I think my family is in danger or needs His protection, not just for life crises and emergencies, and not just for big wishes and dreams, but each and every day for everything. God wants me dependent on him in prayer, trusting him, and walking in faith. I believe God is speaking to me very clearly telling me if I will do that, if I will trust Him, have faith in Him, and be completely dependent on Him, He will use me to accomplish many things.

Along the way, I will receive the blessings and joy of walking with God, knowing I am living and walking in accordance to His will. I believe there is no greater treasure on Earth and in heaven than that relationship with God, and I want it at all costs. I have come to the point in my life where I understand the importance and benefit of trusting God in all things — with my life, my family, my future, with everything. It is an exciting place to be.

I am excited to not have to design a master plan to take over the world, or accomplish God's will the way I think it needs to be accomplished. All I want is to be obedient to the Spirit of God, to hear His voice and to move accordingly, confident and certain in the fact that I am doing God's will and it is His will that matters, not mine. I know His will is better than mine and is for my joy and blessing (Romans 8:28, "and we know that in all things God works for the good of those that love Him, and who are called according to His purpose.") The verse "He must increase but I must decrease" (John 3:30), has never hit me harder, nor has God's instruction that we are to "die to self." This is a challenging but necessary step in reaching the highest level of spiritual growth, spiritual experience, and spiritual awareness we can accomplish while on this Earth. It happens through faithful obedience to God, as we surrender our lives to His will and let Him work through us. It's taken me a long time to get to this point and it shouldn't have. I'm stubborn and selfish and stupid, and I let pride and ego get in my way. But no more. Got has shown me the path and I want to walk down it. Come what may. To God be the glory!

We wish all of you a wonderful and glorious holiday season. We pray over each and every name on our holiday mailing list that the Spirit of God would fill each of you with joy, hope, peace, faith, love, mercy, goodness, kindness, forgiveness, and grace… all of the amazing things that knowing God allows us to do and experience while here on Earth.

Most importantly I pray that each one of you would have individual worship/fellowship/quiet time with God. God says that He is alive, His Word is alive, and He is the Word. I pray that you would take God up on His offer and spend time with Him personally, so He can speak to your heart, mold and shape it so you may experience His joy! As a parent I know and can relate to the fact He only does what He does for your blessing and benefit. We are His children and He loves us so much. Don't miss out on that. It would be tragic.

Wow, what a year! Changes, grandkid, moves, new friends, new opportunity, a whole new chapter in the book of our lives. It shouldn't take all that excitement for you personally to be thrilled about being alive. I think we often take for granted the very gift of life. We hope and pray you see the miracle in each and every day, then not only enjoy it, but embrace it, as well.

God bless you! Have a great holiday and an awesome New Year!

Jack, Beth, Jackson, Talia

YEARGONE – a look back at…

2015

A year of movement. Life was flying by 100 miles an hour. I did everything I could to hang on. Perhaps you've experienced the same. It was **framed beautifully by God putting** special people in my life, a friend **who was dying of cancer and** a cousin with Down Syndrome. Through them God showed me true beauty inside of people's soul's and that what really mattered was people and loving them and receiving their love. It helped me to refocus my purpose, my priorities and what I wanted to be passionate about in my future. Make sure you see that for yourself. If you don't ask God to put you in the middle of a storm so you can see it, or knock you on your butt or do whatever it talks to get your attention and slow you down and open your eyes and your heart so you can see it, because quite simply, it is the key to life and the beauty of life!

FINAL THOUGHTS

Well our time together for this book is gone. Hey that would be a great name for a book…TIME GONE…smile!

I hope I have made you think, as was my goal each and every year when I sent out these holiday letters. I hope I have inspired you to look deep within yourself, at your feelings, what you value, what's important and what you want your life to stand for and how you want to make it count. And as well I hope I've inspired you to take a look outside at the world around you and decide in your own mind for your own self what is good, what is bad, what you want to embrace and what you want to cast away. I think the biggest tragedy of all is people who just go through life without thinking about where they want to go and how they want to get there. Of course they live and eventually die and wonder why they never accomplish the things they wanted too. They never had happiness, joy and peace throughout their life, and I think as God tells us, we are to test ourselves and hold onto what is good.

You know we have our word, which is critical, as people need to be able to count on us to be men and women of integrity. We have our thoughts, and the good news there is, in addition to your relationship with God, no one can take them away from you. I hope above all you are inspired to share your thoughts with others. To dialogue and exchange and not keep them bottled up inside but rather share them as you would love, wisdom and knowledge.

So perhaps this year you write your own holiday letter, sharing with others the love, the truth, wisdom, knowledge and insight you've learned about life. How to live it, how to enjoy it, what's good, what's bad, what can stay the same and what needs to be changed because it doesn't work or it's broken. I think that gift is much more valuable than a Christmas/Holiday card with no personal message that is sent out of routine, just signed with our names or with a family picture. I believe you will be blessed by getting real with yourself and those you know and love. So dig deep, let it out, and of course you can use my own favorite personal theory which is, I write everything down and then edit out what I think is inappropriate to share or just plain stupid... Smile! Keep the train rolling!

www.ingramcontent.com/pod-product-compliance
Lightning Source LLC
Chambersburg PA
CBHW040327300426
44113CB00020B/2681